BYZANTINE WARSHIP
VS
ARAB WARSHIP

7th–11th centuries

ANGUS KONSTAM

First published in Great Britain in 2015 by Osprey Publishing,
PO Box 883, Oxford, OX1 9PL, UK
PO Box 3985, New York, NY 10185-3985, USA
E-mail: info@ospreypublishing.com

Osprey Publishing is part of the Osprey Group

A CIP catalogue record for this book is available from the British Library

Print ISBN: 978 1 4728 0757 1
PDF ebook ISBN: 978 1 4728 0758 8
ePub ebook ISBN: 978 1 4728 0759 5

Index by Mark Swift
Typeset in ITC Conduit and Adobe Garamond
Cover artwork and battlescenes by Peter Dennis
Profile and weaponry artwork by Peter Bull Art Studio
Map by bounford.com
Originated by PDQ Media, Bungay, UK
Printed in China through World Print Ltd

15 16 17 18 19   10 9 8 7 6 5 4 3 2 1

Osprey Publishing is supporting the Woodland Trust, the UK's leading
woodland conservation charity, by funding the dedication of trees.

www.ospreypublishing.com

Author's note

Unless noted otherwise, all illustrations are attributed to the Stratford Archive,
London.

Editor's note

Metric units of measurement are employed in this book. For ease of
comparison please refer to the following conversion table:

1km = 0.62 miles
1m = 1.09yd / 3.28ft
1cm = 0.39in
1mm = 0.04in
1kg = 2.20lb / 35.27oz
1 tonne = 0.98 long (UK) tons / 1.10 short (US) tons

Artist's note

Readers may care to note that the original paintings from which the cover
and battlescenes in this book were prepared are available for private sale. All
reproduction copyright whatsoever is retained by the Publishers. All enquiries
should be addressed to:

Peter Dennis, 'Fieldhead', The Park, Mansfield, Nottinghamshire NG18 2AT, UK,
or email magie.h@ntlworld.com

The Publishers regret that they can enter into no correspondence upon this matter.

CONTENTS

INTRODUCTION

The maritime contest between the Byzantine *dromōn* (pl. *dromōnes*) and the Arab *shalandī* (pl. *shalandiyyat*) began in the mid-7th century and lasted for the best part of four centuries. In their heyday the *dromōn* and *shalandī* fought each other from one end of the Mediterranean to the other. By the mid-11th century, though, a new

In this detail of the well-known Greek Fire image from John Skylitzes' *Synopsis historion*, we see that this very stylized Byzantine *dromōn* is a bireme with a single lateen-rigged mast, and what appears to be a single steering oar. While the bow and stern are both rounded, there is no sign of a spur of any kind. Shields are hung along the side of the vessel.

This depiction of an Arab vessel is an Egyptian graffito of the late 7th century, and shows a small craft fitted with a single mast and lateen sail, steeply sloping bow and stem posts, and what may be a fighting platform in the bow, below the decorative tip of the stem post. It has been suggested that this is an early representation of an Arab *shalandī*, even though the vessel lacks any oars.

form of galley favoured by the Italian city-states – the *galea* – rose to prominence in the Byzantine and Arab navies, and eventually replaced the remaining *dromōnes* and *shalandiyyat*.

The Arab and Byzantine warships owed much to their Roman predecessors in terms of design and fighting potential. Following the collapse of the Western Roman Empire in the 5th century AD, what was once Rome's *mare nostrum* ('our sea') became a naval battleground as barbarian fleets and pirates preyed on Roman shipping. By the 6th century, however, the Byzantines had developed their own powerful navy, which saw off the maritime threat posed by the Vandals and Ostrogoths in the Western Mediterranean, and this fleet spearheaded the revival of Byzantine fortunes during the reign of the Emperor Justinian I (r. 527–65). By the close of the 6th century the Byzantines not only controlled the former Eastern Roman Empire, but had reconquered territory in Italy, North Africa and the Iberian Peninsula as well. While many of these recaptured Roman provinces were little more than narrow strips of territory fringing the coast, Byzantium's powerful fleet served as the glue that bound this largely maritime Empire together. For more than a century, Byzantium was the unchallenged master of the sea, from the Pillars of Hercules (the Strait of Gibraltar) to the Nile Delta.

That all changed in the early 7th century. For centuries the Eastern Roman Empire and its Byzantine successor had waged an intermittent war against the Sassanid Persian Empire. In 611 the Sassanids overran Byzantine Syria, and within nine years they had conquered Egypt and much of Asia Minor. In 626 they even laid siege to Constantinople, but the city defences held, and eventually the Byzantine navy attacked and defeated the Persian fleet and lifted the siege. A Byzantine counter-attack reconquered much of the lost territories in Asia Minor and the Middle East, but the war left the Empire financially and militarily weakened. It was at this crucial moment that a new foe appeared – one that would not just threaten the Byzantine Empire – it would dismember it. While the Byzantines and Persians had been at loggerheads the Islamic prophet Muhammad (*c*.570–*c*.632) emerged as the leader of a militaristic spiritual movement which had captured Mecca, and went on to

During this period Constantinople (now Istanbul) was encircled by formidably high walls, which also covered the seaward side of the city. In this depiction of the 7th- and 8th-century city by Oliver Frey the little harbour on the left is Eleutherios, where the remains of two small Byzantine warships were discovered in 2005, during building work to expand the city's metro system.

conquer most of Arabia. So began what became known as the Arab Conquest – a religiously inspired explosion of military and political power that transformed the known world. While at first the Arabs lacked a navy and found themselves vulnerable to attack from the sea, they soon developed a formidable fleet that confounded Byzantine expectations in the early years of the Arab Conquest – most spectacularly at the 'Battle of the Masts' (*Dhāt al-sawārī*) in 655. The Arabs would prove themselves a doughty adversary over the centuries that followed, making the Romans' unchallenged supremacy in the Mediterranean a distant memory.

Their nature of both *dromōn* and *shalandī* changed substantially over the period. At first they were single-masted monoremes, with limited space for marines and weaponry. These were the galleys that duelled with each other during the 7th and 8th centuries. These monoremes were then superseded by larger versions – bireme galleys with two masts, and more substantial fighting areas on board. These later warships remained in Arab and Byzantine service until the end of our period. Both the *dromōn* and the *shalandī* carried marines as well as oarsmen, whose task was to capture enemy warships by boarding them. However, they also carried a range of missile weapons, from stones and arrows to javelins, darts and large iron bolts. Most dramatically of all, the Byzantines also possessed their great secret weapon – Greek Fire – a highly flammable terror weapon that played a decisive part in the very survival of the Byzantine Empire. The secret was eventually learned by the Arabs, thereby ensuring that naval warfare during this period was a brutal, violent and murderous business. The real stars of this maritime history, though, are the ships themselves – the *dromōnes* and *shalandiyyat* that once dominated the blood-soaked waters of the Mediterranean.

CHRONOLOGY

476 Romulus Augustus (r. 475–76), the last Western Roman Emperor, is deposed.

527–65 The reign of Justinian I: Byzantine forces reconquer much of Imperial Rome's possessions in Africa, Dalmatia, Sicily, Italy and Spain.

602–28 War between the Byzantine Empire and Sassanid Persia leaves both powers gravely weakened; initial Persian success give way to a pyrrhic victory for the Byzantines under Emperor Heraklios (r. 610–41).

632 The Prophet Muhammad dies after conquering Mecca and establishing Islamic rule in the Arabian Peninsula; he is succeeded by the *Rāshidūn* ('Rightly Guided') caliphs (632–61).

634–38 Arab forces conquer Byzantine Syria, winning a decisive victory at Yarmouk (636).

640 Arab victory at Heliopolis heralds the Islamic conquest of Byzantine Egypt.

641 Alexandria, the Egyptian capital, falls to the Arabs; a Byzantine fleet lands troops

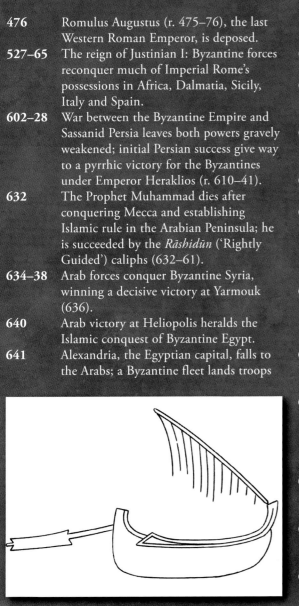

This redrawing of a Byzantine vessel is taken from a manuscript version of the Sermons of St Gregory of Nazianos, produced between 879 and 882. The original is housed in the Bibliothèque nationale de France, Paris. What is most interesting here is the shape of the hull, reminiscent of the 7th-century Yassi Ada wreck, and the clear depiction of the craft's single stern rudder.

that recapture the city in 645, but are defeated by the Arabs at Nikiou in 646.

642/43 Byzantine Tripoli is captured by Arab forces.

647–48 Arab forces briefly invade Byzantine North Africa, defeating local forces before withdrawing.

649 An Arab fleet led by the governor of Syria, Mu'āwiyah ibn Abī Sufyān, raids Byzantine Cyprus.

654 Mu'āwiyah's fleet attacks Byzantine Rhodes.

655 A fleet led by the Arab governor of Egypt, Abdullāh ibn Sa'ad ibn Abī as-Sarh, decisively defeats a larger Byzantine fleet commanded by Constans II 'Pogonatos' (r. 641–68) at the 'Battle of the Masts'.

656–61 Civil war in the Islamic Caliphate, ending with the accession of Mu'āwiyah (r. 661–80) as the founding caliph of the Umayyad Dynasty (661–750).

667 The Arab naval offensive resumes with a raid on Rhodes; the island is captured and briefly held by the Arabs during 673–80.

672–78 A large Arab invasion fleet led by Caliph Mu'āwiyah lands troops outside the walls of Constantinople; the Byzantine capital is besieged, and the Arab fleet lies off the city for six years.

673 Successful Byzantine raid on Alexandria, aimed at damaging the port's shipbuilding capability.

678 First recorded use of Greek Fire in a decisive Byzantine victory in a naval battle off Constantinople.

688 Division of Cyprus between Arabs and Byzantines.

695 The Arabs launch a full-scale invasion of Byzantine North Africa, led by Hasān ibn an-Nu'umān al-Ghasānī (d. *c.*700); Carthage, the regional capital, is besieged and captured once the garrison withdraws to Crete.

A pair of *dromōnes* used to illustrate the margins of the *Sacra Parallela*, a manuscript of the late 9th century attributed to St John of Damascus and now housed in the Bibliothèque nationale de France, Paris. Both vessels are two-masted and carry lateen sails, but strangely they appear to be monoremes rather than biremes.

698	The Emperor Leontios (r. 695–98) counter-attacks Carthage, and his forces briefly recapture the city, only to lose it again following an Arab naval victory just outside the harbour of Carthage. The vulnerability of Carthage to naval assault leads the Arabs to establish a new, more secure naval base in nearby Tunis.
711	Moorish conquest of the Iberian Peninsula begins as the Arabs secure a base on *Jabal Tāriq* (Gibraltar).
716–17	Arab land and sea forces converge on Constantinople; directed by Emperor Leo III 'the Isaurian' (r. 717–41) the Arab fleet is defeated by the Byzantines' use of Greek Fire, but the siege continues.
718	Byzantine victory over Arabs in a second naval battle off Constantinople; the Arab survivors are all but wiped out by a storm as they withdraw.
727	Leo III's fleets quash a rebellion by his Aegean fleet.
747	Byzantine victory over a combined Egyptian and Syrian fleet in a naval battle off Cyprus; Umayyad rule collapses, and that dynasty is replaced by a new Abbasid Caliphate (750–1258).
790	Arab destruction of the *Kibyrrhaiōtai* off Attaleia (now Antalya) on the Mediterranean coast of Asia Minor.
813	Byzantine defeat of an Andalusian Arab invasion force off Palma, in the Balearic Islands.
820–29	The reign of the Emperor Michael II 'the Amorian' is wracked by revolt led by Thomas the Slav (*c.*760–823). Although the central imperial fleet is able to crush this revolt, the Byzantine navy is seriously weakened.
824	The Arab leader Abū Hafs Umar al-Ballūtī (d. *c.*855) lands on Crete and begins his conquest of the island.
826	Ziyādat Allāh I (r. 817–38), a ruler of the Aghlabid Dynasty (800–909), directs an Arab army to land in western Sicily; it fails to take Syracuse thanks to a Byzantine relief expedition.
827	Syracuse is besieged by Arab forces led by Asad ibn al-Furāt (759–828). A Byzantine naval relief attempt is defeated, thanks to

the bolstering of the Arab fleet by Byzantine defectors led by the rebel commander Euphemios.

828 Arab victory over the Byzantines' Aegean thematic fleet off Rethymno, during an Arab assault on the port.

829 The Arabs defeat a Byzantine fleet off the Aegean island of Thasos.

831 The Arabs capture Palermo, Sicily, assisted by the defection of Euphemios, *droungarios* of the Sicilian thematic fleet.

840 An Arab invasion fleet sent from Sicily to Calabria defeats a combined Byzantine and Venetian fleet off Punta Stilo. This is followed by a large-scale Arab invasion of Calabria and Apulia.

841 An Arab fleet raiding deep into the northern Adriatic defeats the local Byzantine fleet off Spalato (now Split).

842 The Arab fleet operating off southern Italy is defeated in the Bay of Naples by a combined Byzantine and Italian Lombard fleet.

843 Messina falls to the Aghlabids, and with it they gain control of the narrow straits separating Sicily from the Italian mainland. Syracuse is captured in 878, and Arab control over the island is finally complete by 907.

846 An Arab fleet appears off Ostia – the port serving Rome – and the Byzantines are unable to protect the city.

853 Successful Byzantine raid on Damietta, Egypt.

858 A combined Byzantine and Venetian fleet is repulsed during a naval assault on the Arab-held port of Taranto.

860 Byzantine defeat of the Rus' (Slavic invaders from modern Russia) outside Constantinople; reinforcements are sent north to protect the Empire's northern borders.

867 An Arab raid on Ragusa (now Dubrovnik) is repulsed by the Byzantine thematic fleet operating in the Adriatic.

868 A Byzantine fleet attempting to lift the Arab siege of Syracuse is defeated.

868 Niketas Oöryphas (*fl.*860–73), *droungarios tou ploïmou*, drags a small Byzantine fleet across the Isthmus of Corinth and attacks an Aghlabid fleet operating in the Southern Adriatic. The Arabs are routed, and Byzantine maritime dominance is restored in the Southern Adriatic.

878 Arab capture of Syracuse, Sicily.

879 A Byzantine naval expedition inflicts a major defeat on the Cretan Arabs, which restores Byzantine control over the Mediterranean and curtails large-scale Cretan raids until the end of the century.

879 An Arab raiding fleet from Sicily is cornered and destroyed in the Bay of Naples by a combined Byzantine imperial and thematic fleet.

880 A small Byzantine detachment sent into the Aegean to support the recapture of several of the Ionian Islands encounters a Sicilian Arab fleet off the island of Corfu; the use of Greek Fire proves decisive in the Byzantine victory.

888 A Sicilian Arab fleet wins a decisive victory in the battle of Milazzo, Sicily, effectively ending Byzantine naval influence in the Western Mediterranean for the next three decades, and empowering the Sicilian Arabs to raid further east.

c.889 An Arab fleet from the Umayyad Emirate in Iberia establishes a base at Fraxinetum (now La Garde-Freinet on the French Mediterranean coast) and begins to mount raids in the region, effectively depriving the Byzantines of large areas of their empire.

904 An Arab fleet led by the corsair Leo of Tunis, a Greek renegade, sacks the Byzantine city of Thessaloniki and then escapes to the east, operating as privateers from bases in northern Syria. Leo's galleys continue to dominate the Aegean basin until his defeat off Lemnos in 923.

909 Abdullāh al-Mahdī Billah (r. 909–34) establishes the Fātimid Dynasty in North Africa, a rival to the Abbasid Caliphate.

911 The Byzantines send a large expeditionary force to Crete, but it is forced to withdraw and is largely destroyed by the Syrian fleet at the battle of Chios.

920–44	Reign of Emperor Romanos I Lekapenos; he reorganizes the fleet and introduces larger and more powerful *dromōnes*, aiding the Byzantine reclamation of the Eastern Mediterranean, formerly a maritime no man's land.
941	Romanos I defeats a large Rus' fleet led by Igor I, Prince of Kiev (r. 914–45), thereby safeguarding the Black Sea approaches to the Byzantine capital and allowing the redeployment of naval resources to the Mediterranean.
949	Emperor Constantine VII 'Porphyrogennetos' (r. 908–59) mounts an ultimately unsuccessful amphibious expedition to Crete, leaving a detailed bureaucratic legacy.
956	Byzantine forces recapture Naples after Byzantine fleets are sent back into Italian waters in support of land operations.
960	The Byzantines send a second amphibious force to Crete, recapturing the island and depriving the Arabs of a base that had posed a major threat to Byzantine control of the Aegean for the past 130 years.
963	The Arab fleet based in Cyprus is destroyed off Larnaca by the combined *Karabisianoi* and *Kibyrrhaiōtai* during the Byzantine reconquest of the island by Emperor Nikephoros II Phokas (r. 963–69).
965	Byzantine reconquest of Cyprus.
965	Following the landing of a Byzantine expeditionary force on the east coast of Sicily, the Byzantine fleet is ambushed and largely destroyed by the returning Fātimid fleet; Byzantine operations in the region are halted.
965	Byzantine forces led by Nikephoros II Phokas capture the major Arab port of Tarsus, presaging an even more ambitious Byzantine assault on the Syrian coast.
972	The privateering lair at Fraxinetum is captured by a coalition of Christian forces; in ensuing decades Italian and other naval forces resist and overcome Arab fleets in the Central Mediterranean, clearing the Tyrrhenian Sea of Moorish privateers and capturing Corsica in 1016.
975	A Byzantine raid on Beirut is repulsed with heavy losses.

998	Naval battle off Tyre ends in a Fātimid victory over a Byzantine force attempting to reinforce the defenders of that city.
999	Emperor Basil II 'Boulgaroktonos' (r. 976–1025) and the Fātimid caliph, Abu Ali Mansur Tāriqu al-Hākim (r. 996–1021), sign a peace treaty, ending the long and largely inconclusive war.
1025	Attempted Byzantine invasion of Sicily; the Fātimid fleet sent to intercept the Byzantines is largely destroyed in a storm but in the end the expedition proves unsuccessful.
1035	The *Kibyrrhaiōtai* destroy a Syrian Arab raiding fleet off the Lycian coast as it returns home laden with plunder, after a successful incursion into the Aegean.
1043	Naval battle in Bosporus – Byzantine victory over Rus' forces.
1071	The battle of Manzikert – Seljuk Turkish victory over a Byzantine army.

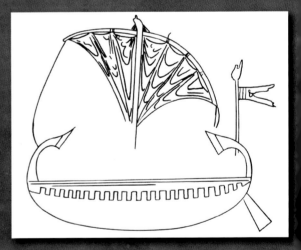

This reproduction of an Arab manuscript illustration from the *Maqamat al-Harīrī* by al-Harīrī (1054–1122) shows a Syrian sailing ship of the early 13th century. While later than our time period, it shows several features which would have been present in earlier Arab *shalandiyyat*. These include the recurved stem and stern post decoration, the lateen sail hung from a hooked masthead, and a rather enigmatic banner in the stern, flown from a pole surmounted by some form of ornate finial.

THE STRATEGIC SITUATION

THE MEDITERRANEAN BATTLEGROUND

The *dromōn* and the *shalandī* were developed in order to operate in a specific setting – the Mediterranean. Naval warfare in the Mediterranean during the Early Medieval period was dominated by three things: sea lanes, islands and bases. All of the major battles fought between the Arab and Byzantine fleets during this era took place somewhere along the major maritime arteries that spanned the Mediterranean Sea. These ran from Egypt north along the Levantine coast to Syria, then east past Cyprus, following the coast of Asia Minor as far as the Aegean. The island of Crete served as a stopper to the Aegean bottle, and so Levantine trade passed to the east of the island, and occidental trade passed it to the west. From there the sea lanes crossed the base of the Adriatic to reach the southern coast of Italy, and then continued on to Sicily and the Byzantine province of Africa (now Tunisia). Beyond Sicily trade routes spread westwards towards the Balearic Islands and the Iberian Peninsula. Both Arab and Byzantine strategists understood the economic and political importance of maintaining control of these sea lanes. That was why control of the islands of Cyprus, Crete and Sicily remained of paramount importance to both sides. Not only could fleets based there interdict these sea lanes, but their geographical presence created maritime bottlenecks, which dictated the shape of almost all of these naval campaigns. In the

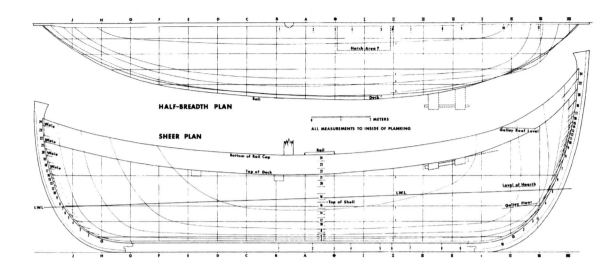

ABOVE The hull lines of the 7th-century Byzantine merchant vessel discovered off Yassi Ada, reconstructed from an analysis of her surviving timbers, after its underwater excavation during the early 1960s. The profile is typical of many Mediterranean vessels of our period, including some of the larger Arab *shalandiyyat* of the later 8th century onwards, with the exception that these galleys had a considerably narrower beam than this merchant vessel.

late 10th century the Arab writer Muhammad ibn Ahmad Shams al-Dīn al-Muqaddasī (*c*.945–91) made this point with admirable clarity:

> In this sea there are three flourishing and well-populated islands. One is Sicily ... then there is Crete ... and then Cyprus. The sea has two channels, which are well known, and on its coast are many towns and important fortresses and excellent *ribats* [anchorages]. The people who are in control of the sea are the *Rum* [Byzantines], and they very much impose their fear on the sea ... And in this sea are the routes to Syria and Egypt. (Quoted in Pryor 1988: 107)

The design and development of the *dromōn* and the *shalandī* would be shaped by this setting, but their strengths and limitations would help to define the nature of the war at sea between the Byzantines and the Arabs in this period. The most significant aspect of galley warfare was that these warships weren't capable of conducting long-distance operations. They had limited storage facilities, and so they were unable to operate for more than a week or so without needing to return to a friendly base to replenish their supplies of food and water. Galleys tended to operate within sight of land, and in most

instances they would put into shore at nightfall, and resume their voyage in the morning. This made the presence of bases and friendly coastlines of paramount importance in these naval campaigns. The naval battles of this period tended to take place in limited geographical areas – for instance the waters around Cyprus, the southern coast of Asia Minor, the sea approaches to Constantinople, the southern coast of Italy, and off the northern and eastern coasts of Sicily. In almost every case they were fought to determine control of ports, areas of coastline and strategically important islands. These were the locations where victory or defeat in this great struggle would be determined.

THE SITUATION IN THE 7TH CENTURY

At the opening of our period the Mediterranean was convulsed by rapid and violent change. In 634 the first Arab incursions had begun on the Byzantine Empire's southern frontier in Egypt and Syria. By the end of the year the Arabs were in Damascus, helped by the ill health of the warlike Emperor Heraklios (r. 610–41). The decisive Arab victory at Yarmouk (636) led to the conquest of Syria, and soon Egypt and Mesopotamia were also wrested from Byzantine control. By 642 Alexandria had fallen to the Arabs, which meant they controlled the entire coast of Egypt and Syria, and so gained access to several major ports. This rapid collapse of Byzantine power in the Middle East didn't alter the naval situation in the Mediterranean – at least not immediately. Certainly, the Byzantines lost control of important naval bases and shipbuilding ports such as Alexandria, Acre, Tyre and St Symeon (the port serving Antioch), but Byzantine domination of the Mediterranean was unchallenged. What had begun as a military conquest would now take on a naval aspect, however, as the Byzantine navy did what it could to stem the Arab advance. The Arabs were utter 'landlubbers', but the 'Rightly Guided Caliphs' who succeeded Muhammad as leaders of the Arab *jihād* ('struggle') quickly realized the strategic importance of sea power. Much of the economy of the Arabs' newly acquired provinces depended on maritime trade, which was strangled thanks to the Byzantine naval presence. In 645 a Byzantine naval attack on Alexandria, Egypt, demonstrated the Arab vulnerability to attack from the sea.

There were only two ways the Arabs could break this maritime stranglehold. One was by denying the Byzantines naval bases from which to operate, much as Alexander the

In the early part of our period Byzantine control of the seas allowed them to land forces anywhere along the Arab-held coast, meaning that Arab military strength had to be diluted to maintain large garrisons and defensive armies. Here, Arabs slaughter a Byzantine invasion force during one of several Byzantine attempts to recapture Crete. The Byzantine *dromōnes* in the illumination have twin stern posts, twin steering oars, and small spurs. This makes them contemporaneous with the manuscript, produced around 1160, rather than typical of the *dromōnes* in use during the early 9th century. From the *Synopsis historion* by John Skylitzes.

OPPOSITE This crude depiction of a vessel comes from a wall painting in Egypt from the late 5th or early 6th centuries. It therefore shows a vessel in use in Egypt when the region still formed part of the Byzantine Empire. It is probably a warship, as it carries a spur at the bow, and is fitted with a single lateen sail. However, no oars are shown. Its similarity to earlier Egyptian vessels is noticeable, and indicates the continued presence of a strong regional shipbuilding tradition in Byzantine Egypt.

13

A pair of Byzantine *dromōnes* in a detail of a larger illustration from John Skylitzes' *Synopsis historion*. These are clearly meant to represent biremes, and show one or two helmsmen in the stern, and a decorative recurve at the top of the stem post.

OPPOSITE Although it began in the east, the naval campaign between the Arabs and the Byzantines was fought out across the whole length of the Mediterranean Sea. Byzantine fortunes fluctuated during this period – most notably in the 9th century when the Empire lost control of the key islands of Crete and Sicily. The dates shown here indicate that full-scale naval battles were a rarity during this period. More common were small-scale operations such as raids on enemy-held ports, islands or coastlines, privateering attacks and naval skirmishes. A combination of geography and logistics dictated the location and pace of the fighting. Most battles were fought along the main trade arteries of the Mediterranean, and the limited range of war galleys meant that the rival fleets needed secure coastlines or bases from which to operate. The naval war was therefore one that centred on the control of islands and ports, and the domination of key trading routes.

Great had done during his campaign against the Persian Empire in the 4th century BC. The other – and ultimately the more successful – was the building of a galley fleet capable of wresting control of the Eastern Mediterranean from the Byzantines, and thereby seizing the strategic initiative. While the Arabs had little experience of Mediterranean shipbuilding, their newly conquered territories included ports with shipbuilding facilities – ones which the Byzantines had used to build their own galleys. This meant they had immediate access to shipbuilding facilities and expertise, and so were able to draw upon this when they began building their own fleet. So, as Arab armies continued their advance along the North African coast, shipwrights in the newly conquered territories were directed to begin building a fleet that could challenge the supremacy of Byzantine sea power. By 649 they were ready to challenge the Byzantines. That year the governor of Syria, Mu'āwiyah ibn Abī Sufyān, launched a raid against Cyprus, destroying the ancient city of Salamis. An Arab attack on Rhodes followed, and in 655 a fleet led by the Arab governor of Egypt, Abdullāh ibn Sa'ad ibn Abī as-Sarh (d. 656), clashed off Cape Chelidonya in Lycia (south-eastern Asia Minor) with a larger Byzantine fleet commanded by the Byzantine Emperor himself, Constans II, at the 'Battle of the Masts' – an encounter that would transform the naval balance of power in the Mediterranean.

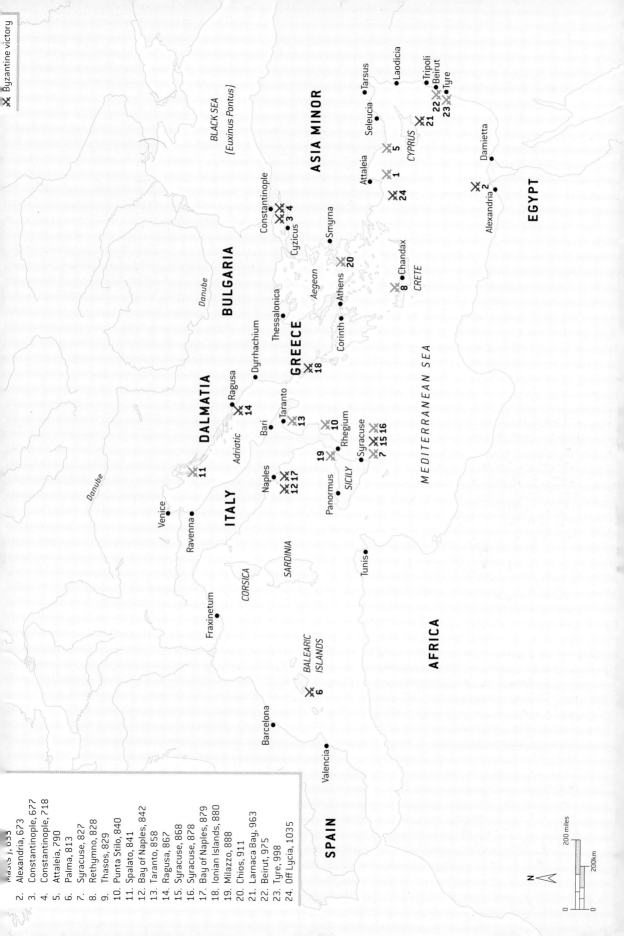

✗ Byzantine victory

BLACK SEA
(Euxinus Pontus)

ASIA MINOR

Laodicia
Tarsus
Tripoli
Beirut
Tyre
Seleucia
Attaleia
CYPRUS
Damietta
Alexandria
EGYPT

Constantinople
Cyzicus
Smyrna
Athens
Chandax
CRETE

BULGARIA

Danube

Thessalonica
Durrhachium
GREECE
Corinth

Aegean

Ragusa
DALMATIA
Bari
Taranto
Rhegium
Syracuse
SICILY
Panormus
Naples
Venice
Ravenna
ITALY
Adriatic

MEDITERRANEAN SEA

Danube

Fraxinetum
CORSICA
SARDINIA
Tunis
AFRICA

Barcelona
BALEARIC ISLANDS
Valencia
SPAIN

N

0   200 miles
0   200km

DESIGN AND DEVELOPMENT

So what did the vessels that fought at the Battle of the Masts look like, and how did their design and fighting methods address the challenges of fighting in the Mediterranean setting? In fact, the opposing fleets at the battle are likely to have looked very similar. Modern scholars (Gardiner 1995, Pryor & Jeffreys 2006) suggest that the Arab vessels were largely indistinguishable from their Byzantine counterparts. Any modifications to incorporate distinctly Arabic features would be incorporated into this Byzantine-style design over time. Both sides' vessels were designed, constructed and – in the Arab case, only partly – manned by members of traditional seafaring communities who drew upon a longstanding tradition of shipbuilding and seamanship within the Roman world.

A SHARED LEGACY

Before the demise of the Western Roman Empire the Roman navy had little need for powerful warships. The Roman Republic's naval conflicts against Carthage or the Greek and Macedonian states had been won long ago; as the sole naval power in the Mediterranean Rome had no need for fleets of large warships, and so these great multibanked war galleys were scrapped, and replaced by a new breed of small warships, whose job was to help police Rome's frontiers, and to deal with any threat from pirates. For the most part these small warships were of a type known as the *liburna* (pl. *liburnae*)

A detail of a bas-relief from Pozzuoli in Italy, showing a Roman warship of the early 1st century AD. This vessel appears to be a bireme, with a twin steering oar, a ram in her prow, and highly decorated stem and stern posts. This was a *liburna*, the forerunner of the Byzantine *dromōn*.

– a small, fast open-decked galley with one or two banks of oars. These *liburnae* were supported by a small number of triremes of a type known as the *triērēs* (pl. *triēreis*), and a mere handful of larger galleys with four, five or six banks of oars, retained to serve as fleet flagships more for purposes of prestige than practicality. The *triēreis* proved useful when launching punitive expeditions against any pirate lairs, but the Roman warship par excellence was the *liburna*. It was the patrol ship of the day, equally useful chasing pirate ships as escorting merchantmen through pirate waters, or scouting ahead of a naval force.

The *liburna* was named after the Liburnians, the Late Hellenistic inhabitants of the Dalmatian coast, who in the 1st century BC had developed a fast light galley known as a *lembos* (pl. *lemboi*). The design was adapted for use by the Roman navy by abandoning the outrigger (*apostis*) which supported the bireme's oars. Instead, the naval *liburna* had oar ports cut in the hull itself, which gave the vessel a sleeker appearance than its predecessor. A box-like casing covered the oar ports, offering some protection from a raking attack when the *liburna* went into action. These naval *liburnae* also had a lower hull configuration than their predecessors, while a fighting platform was added by way of a forecastle. Usually, some form of superstructure – temporary or otherwise – was added at the stern to accommodate the warship's captain. These Roman warships were primarily used to overhaul pirates and capture them by boarding. To this end they carried a complement of marines and missile troops. When it was first developed the *liburna* was fitted with a ram, which meant that it could be used as a weapon in its own right. The *liburna* remained the primary naval vessel of the Roman navy for more than four centuries. Although pictorial evidence suggests the *liburna* may have undergone minor changes during this period, its basic design remained unaltered.

While these small galleys were ideally suited to their role, they were not designed to fight in a large-scale naval action. So, in AD 267, when a fleet of Gothic war

A *liburna*, depicted in a 3rd-century mosaic portraying the voyage of the *Odyssey*, from a Roman villa in Dougga in present-day Tunisia. The ram bow is clearly visible here, as is the protective box covering the oar ports, the mainmast fitted with a square sail, and a small foremast. All are features which changed following the evolution of the *dromōn*.

galleys brushed aside the naval defences of the Bosporus and entered the Aegean Sea, the Romans were initially unable to stop them. Eventually the Gothic fleet was defeated in a surprise amphibious attack, but the point was made – if similar incursions were to be avoided, then more powerful warships would be needed to bolster the Empire's naval defences. By 324, during a war against his rival, the co-Emperor Licinius I (r. 308–24), the Emperor Constantine I 'the Great' (r. 324–37) – the founder of Constantinople – successfully commanded a large fleet of *triēreis* and smaller, 30-oared warships of a type called the *triakontērēs* (pl. *triakontoroi*). While this mention of triremes shows that large vessels were still being built, the 30-oared ship was presumably a smaller and faster form of vessel. In 399 an attempted Gothic crossing of the Hellespont (Dardanelles) was thwarted by a fleet of Late Roman *liburnae*, which suggests these vessels were still guarding Rome's maritime borders. It is from this period – around the time of the fall of the Western Roman Empire – that the *dromōn* is first mentioned, in a fragment of text tentatively attributed to the Greek historian Eunapius of Sardis (349–*c*.414). It described the employment of 30-oared warships known as *dromades*, built in the form of *liburnae*. The implication is that these 30-oared vessels were a new variant of the *liburna*.

Warships belonging to the Eastern Roman Empire – by now effectively the Byzantine Empire – continued to protect the reduced boundaries of the empire against incursions from the Vandals to the west and the Goths to the north. Unfortunately, no clear description of warships survives from this period – all we have are a few pictorial depictions of the warships which formed the core of the early Byzantine navy. What they show is that there was no dramatic change in warship design during the 4th and 5th centuries. Instead, it appears that the Late Roman tradition of relying on *liburnae* continued, and these warships formed the core of the Byzantine fleets of the Justinian Dynasty (518–602).

THE *DROMŌN*

The name *dromōn* appears all too infrequently in Early Byzantine sources. It is only in the 6th century that the term appears with any regularity. What becomes clear is that the term *liburna* remained in use for some time after the fall of the Western Roman Empire, and while it was similar to the *dromōn*, it was somehow slightly different. The term *dromōn* comes from the Greek word *dromos* ('to race'). The inference is that a *dromōn* was a type of galley that was faster than a standard *liburna*. In the 550s the historian Procopius of Caesarea (*c*.500–*c*.565) underlined this characteristic in his description of the *dromōnes* sent by General Flavius Belisarius (*c*.505–*c*.565) to Africa in 533:

DROMŌN, MID-7TH CENTURY

The first recorded *dromōnes* were monoreme galleys, fitted with a single mainmast, rigged with a yard carrying a lateen sail. By the later 6th century, bireme *dromōnes* are mentioned in the sources. This reconstruction is based on one of these larger galleys, where the lower bank of oars was completely protected by a full deck. The upper tier of oarsmen sat on thwarts placed on this deck, and were partially protected by a bulwark. A small fighting platform was located in the bow, behind the curving stem post, and the narrow spur which was used to help the galley ride up over the oars or hull sides of its opponents. The mast was designed to be lowered, by unshipping it from the mast step, and laying it on one or two mast steps. In the stern, one – or more likely two – steering oars flanked a central small cabin structure.

… they were single-banked ships covered by decks, in order that the men rowing them might if possible not be exposed to the bolts of the enemy. Such ships are called *dromōnes* by those of the present time; for they are able to attain a great speed. In these [92 galleys] sailed two thousand men of Byzantium, who were all rowers as well as fighting men, for there was not a single superfluous man among them. (Quoted in Pryor & Jeffreys 2006: 126)

The inference, though, is not that the *dromōn* emerged during the early Byzantine period as a new design in its own right. Instead, it evolved from the *liburna* over time, and the term was used to refer to *liburnae* that were particularly speedy. However, by the mid-6th century the term *dromōn* was used in reference to a variant of the *liburna* – a small, fast war galley that was fully decked and had a crew of about 50 oarsmen. Other characteristics have also begun to appear, as evidenced by the few contemporary depictions of these *dromōnes*. They carried lateen sails, rather than the square sails favoured by *liburnae*. Finally the waterline ram carried by the *liburna* for more than half a millennium had been replaced by a spur, mounted above the waterline. The bow was also more lightly constructed than that of the older *liburna*, as without the need to bear the strength needed to support a working ram, the stem could be slimmer, and designed more for speed than strength. The increasing use of the term *dromōn* during the 6th century is mirrored by a decline in references to the *liburna*. By the start of the 7th century the older term had fallen into disuse. From that point on, all Byzantine war galleys were referred to as *dromōnes*. So, while the *dromōn* appears to have its origins as a form of *liburna*, by 600 it had completely replaced its progenitor as the archetypal war galley of the Byzantine Empire. Together, the decked hull, the use of a spur rather than a ram, and the lateen-rigged sail configuration defined the *dromōn* from the era of the Justinian Dynasty, through the brief reign of the Emperor Phokas (602–10) and the rulers of the Heraclian Dynasty (610–711) who followed him. These were the *dromōnes* that had established Byzantine control over the Mediterranean, and which faced the new challenge posed by the creation of an Arab fleet in the mid-7th century.

The Byzantine *dromōnes* that first met the challenge posed by the Arabs were fast, relatively light galleys, either monoremes or possibly biremes, with a curved spur at the bow, and fitted with a single mast, from which a lateen sail was rigged. These craft represented a delicate balance between speed, seaworthiness and combat potential. The fact that they dominated the Mediterranean for a century before the rise of the Arab

DROMŌN, LATE 9TH CENTURY

At some time during the 8th century two-masted *dromōnes* began to appear, a development which greatly improved the sailing performance of these ships. The size of the vessel didn't increase dramatically, as oar benches were still limited to an effective maximum of around 25 per bank. That meant that like earlier bireme *dromōnes*, these galleys were powered by approximately 100 oars, mounted in two banks. What did change was the fighting potential of the *dromōn*, which now boasted a fighting platform amidships, located between the masts, as well as an enlarged fighting platform in the bow. In *dromōnes* of the *Karabisianoi*, a Greek Fire siphon was located below this forward platform, which protected the siphon crew from enemy missile fire. The slender spur remained, but the shape of the stem and stern posts became increasingly curved from the 9th century onwards.

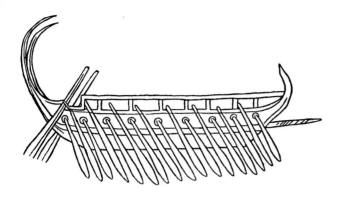

In this line rendition of a graffito, a Byzantine bireme *dromōn* of the 11th or 12th centuries is depicted, with its inward curving twin stem posts, a spur at its bow, and two steering oars. In many ways this graffito is one of the more accurate depictions of a Byzantine *dromōn* of the second half of our period. Drawing based on a *dromōn* depicted in a 12th-century Byzantine illustrated manuscript, now housed in the Bibliothèque nationale de France, Paris.

challenge demonstrated just how effective these galleys had become. It is clear that by the mid- to late 8th century a new type of *dromōn* had evolved, matched by a similar development of the Arab *shalandī*. This new generation of war galleys were considerably more effective than those described above. Under the supervision of the Emperor Rōmanos I Lakapēnos (r. 920–44) the Byzantine navy was overhauled, larger and more powerful *dromōnes* were built, and the fleet was expanded. In this, their final development, these warships would reach the peak of their fighting potential.

What is surprising is the lack of Byzantine references to different types of galley. The terms *ousiakos*, *pamphylos* (or *pamphylion*) and *chelandion* are all mentioned in Byzantine records, and all are referred to as *dromōnes*, without any clear indication of why they were grouped together in some accounts, and divided into smaller groups in others. However, when looking a little more closely at the records we find that the *ousiakos* was crewed by a single *ousia* (pl. *ousiai*) – a Byzantine crewing unit equivalent to a little over 100 men. It is also recorded as having 100 oars, which means the vessel was powered by one man per oar, in two banks. This made it a bireme which appears similar to the larger *dromōnes* that entered service from the late 8th century onwards. The *pamphylos* carried one-and-a-half *ousiai*, but retained the same number of oars. Either some oars were pulled by two oarsmen, or – a more likely option – the extra men served as marines.

The *chelandion* – a name from which the Arab *shalandī* is probably derived – carried three *ousiai*, but again it was a 100-oar bireme – so again, either more than one man worked each oar, or else the vessel was a floating barracks, filled with marines. Interestingly, by the 10th century the term *chelandion* was often used interchangeably with *dromōn*, suggesting that the two terms were synonymous. The inference is that these galleys were all fairly similar, as the number of oars pretty much dictates the size of the vessel. What varied was the size of the crew – a subject that will be discussed later.

The only Byzantine war galley which seem to be classed separately because they represented a different type of vessel was the *monērēs* (pl. *monēreis*) – the descendant of the older monoreme *dromōnes* of the earlier Byzantine period. These had 50 oars per vessel, served by half an *ousia*. While the documentary evidence suggests these craft took part in naval battles, they were probably considered more useful as scouting vessels. Another term which is sometimes used for them is the *dromonion* (or *dromonarion*), a diminutive form of the term *dromōn*. This underlines the assumption that these vessels were *dromōnes* – only smaller versions of the large biremes which now formed the core of the Byzantine fleet. The *monērēs* eventually evolved into the vessel type known as the *galea*, a fast, light craft that was widely adopted by the navies of the Italian city-states from the 11th century onwards. Eventually it would come to replace both the *dromōn* and the *shalandī* as the archetypal warship of the Mediterranean.

In summary, a typical large *dromōn* during the era of the Macedonian Dynasty would be a bireme, fitted with two masts, carrying lateen sails. It would have a spur at the bow, and fighting platforms both at the bow and amidships. It would be about 28m long, and

SHALANDĪ, MID-7TH CENTURY

When the Arabs first began building a galley fleet in the mid-7th century they drew on the shipbuilding traditions and peoples of the seafaring communities of Syria and Egypt. The Coptic (Egyptian Christian) seafarers of Alexandria and Damietta had been building ships for their Byzantine masters, and did the same for their new rulers. They also adapted the warships they produced to suit the needs of the Arabs, who placed a greater emphasis on the use of marines than did the Byzantines, as the Arabs felt they couldn't wholly rely on their Coptic oarsmen. What little we can glean from various sources suggests that 7th-century Arab galleys – *shalandiyyat* – were higher-sided than their Byzantine counterparts, to create a better fighting platform. These craft were either monoreme or bireme galleys – both types are mentioned – with full decks covering the lower tier of oarsmen. These vessels were single-masted, and rigged with a single lateen sail.

would be propelled by around 50 oars per side, in two banks. While a number of monoreme *dromōnes* were still employed in the fleet, these were probably consigned to the fringes of the battle line during a large-scale naval action. Whatever form it took, the Byzantine *dromōn* of this period was a fast, manoeuvrable, well-armed and potentially deadly form of warship. For several centuries it was the floating epitome of Byzantine naval power.

THE *SHALANDĪ*

An Arab merchant vessel, operating in the Red Sea or the Persian Gulf, from an Arab illumination dated to around the 13th century. Of interest is the shape of the hull – similar to those of later Egyptian or Syrian *shalandiyyat* – the fixtures and fittings such as the shape of the anchor, and the dress and appearance of the Arab sailors.

A ceramic bowl in Cairo's Museum of Islamic Art dating from the 10th century shows a monoreme galley with 16 oars per side, with both stem post and stern post curving sharply upwards, no sign of a spur at the bow, and a single mast amidships, carrying a large lateen sail. It is generally assumed that this represents a typical Arabic *shalandī* of the centuries immediately following the Arab Conquest. Just like that of the Byzantine *dromōn*, the appearance of the Arab *shalandī* changed over time. From the start of the 8th century on there was a tendency to build two distinct types of *shalandī* – larger and more powerful bireme galleys, and smaller and more nimble monoreme ones. Lighter *shalandiyyat* were used for amphibious raids, to scout out the enemy, and to protect the sea lanes, while larger and heavier *shalandiyyat* probably formed the core of the main battle fleets, whose primary purpose was to engage the Byzantine fleet in battle.

What the Arabs called their warships is open to some debate, made considerably more complicated by the fact that the compilers of their maritime records used Greek, not Arabic. In the early 8th century, Greek clerks working for the Arab administration in Egypt used the term *dromonarion* (pl. *dromonarium*) in reference to the galleys of their own fleet, while the terms *akation* and *karabion* (pl. *karaboi*) were also employed. The first term is self-explanatory – a reference to an Egyptian *dromōn* – while *akation* referred to a light merchant galley, and a *karabion* was a form of bireme. The *karabion* used by the Arabs was also referred to by the Byzantines as a *dieres* ('two' – a bireme), while the Byzantines used the terms *koumbarion* and *satouraon* to refer to the larger and smaller *shalandī* variants respectively. The *koumbarion* was the same *karabion* ship type listed by those 8th-century Greek clerks, who referred to some of these *dromonarium* and *karaboi* as *kastellatoi* ('castellated' or – more accurately – fitted with fighting platforms).

24

SHALANDĪ, MID-9TH CENTURY

The tendency to build Arab warships with higher sides than their Byzantine counterparts led to the development of the *musattah*. This variant of the *shalandī* was a bireme galley, fitted with two masts, each carrying a large lateen sail. As with Byzantine galleys these masts could be unshipped when required – usually before battle commenced – and were laid out along the deck, supported on mast crutches. Unlike on Byzantine warships, it appears this could be done at the deck level. Arab sources mention that fighting platforms were integral to the hull structure, and were located in the bow, and amidships. The stern area was also raised up slightly above the main deck, presumably to protect the two stern oars, one carried on each quarter. If catapults or naphtha throwers developed from Greek Fire siphons were carried, they would have been mounted in the bow platform, with lighter projectile weapons carried amidships.

This partial depiction of an Arab galley comes from a 13th-century parchment fragment in the Museum of Islamic Art in Cairo, but it shows the stern of an earlier Arab *shalandī*, with a single bank of oars, a decoratively curved stern post, and what looks like a single steering oar on the starboard quarter. Armed Arab warriors stand on the deck, while below them the hull sides give the impression of being painted or decorated in some manner.

The Arab terms for *karabion* include *qādis* (pl. *qawādis*) or *qārib* (pl. *qawārib*). By the 8th century it appears that these biremes formed a major part of the Egyptian fleet. In Arab sources the term *ghurāb* (pl. *aghriba*) is widely used as a generic term for a galley, although the term became more specific in the 10th century. The word *shīnī* (pl. *shawānī*) referred to a war galley, but again at least initially this was a generic term, covering all naval galleys in Arab service. More specifically, the term *shalandī* was first used in Egypt during the 7th century to refer to Byzantine *dromōnes*, but it soon came to encompass their Arab counterparts. The equivalent Byzantine term was *chelandion* (pl. *chelandia*), which interestingly was first used to refer to horse transports, then fast monoreme *dromōnes*, and was eventually used in reference to both Byzantine and Arab war galleys. This suggests that the Arab version of the term was adopted to refer to Byzantine galleys, and was then used interchangeably by the Arabs to mean both Byzantine and Arab *dromōn*-type galleys.

To add to the confusion, the Arab term *marākib* was frequently used as a generic term for 'ship', while in his 10th-century work *Kitāb Sūrat al-arḍ*, the Arab scholar Muhammad Abū'l-Qāsim Ibn Hawqal (fl. 943–78) used the terms *dromun* and *shalandī* as generic terms for both Arab and Byzantine war galleys. The Byzantines also added to the nomenclature problem – for instance, in a letter written in 811 by the Byzantine scholar Theophanes the Confessor (*c.*759–817), an Arab fleet was described as consisting of *dromōnes* and grain-carrying *katēnai* (transport ships). Although the terms *dromōn* and *shalandī* appear to have been interchangeable, for the sake of clarity we shall use the former term to refer to Byzantine galleys, and the latter to their Arab counterparts.

By the 10th century the Arabs were using the term *shīnī* to refer to the smaller monoreme or bireme version of the *shalandī*, while the term *musattah* (pl. *musattahāt*) or sometimes the more generic *ghurāb* encompassed the larger version of the *shalandī*. Another variant worth noting here was the *harrāqa* (pl. *harrāqat*), or 'fire ship', which was developed to counter Byzantine warships equipped with Greek Fire. One enigmatic reference mentions a much larger vessel. The Persian geographer Nāsir Khusraw Qubādiyānī (1004–88) mentioned seeing the remains of an enormous galley, one that once belonged to the Fātimid Caliph Ma'ādh Abū Tamīm al-Mu'izz li Dīn Allāh (r. 953–75). If he is to be believed it was approximately 85m long, with a beam of 35m. This seems impossibly large, and so the assumption is that if the dimensions are correct, this vessel was a purpose-built craft, probably constructed as a floating siege platform, or for some similar engineering purpose. However, it merely emphasizes the fact that the Arab fleet was large, varied and versatile.

TECHNICAL
SPECIFICATIONS

INTERPRETING THE SOURCES

The discoveries of maritime archaeology are frustratingly meagre for this period. At the time of writing only two warships of the period have been discovered, in what was once one of the harbours of Constantinople. They were just small patrol craft, and while they reveal a little about the way Byzantine warships were built, they add little to our understanding of the *dromōn* and the *shalandī*. One can only hope that maritime archaeology will provide us with more information about these vessels in the future.

Unfortunately, the documentary and iconographic evidence of these important warships is also limited, particularly so in the case of the Arab vessels. To understand how these two naval rivals fought each other we have to turn to a limited number of contemporary treatises and records, most of which were written from the Byzantine perspective. From the late 9th century onwards there is a dramatic increase in the availability of information about the war galleys used by the two protagonists in the Eastern Mediterranean. This is particularly true for the *dromōn*,

Although the 'Kyrenia Ship', dating from the 4th century BC, is much older than the vessels described here, this view of her remains clearly demonstrate the 'shell first' construction techniques used to build her. This technique remained in use in the Mediterranean throughout our period, although shipbuilders placed an increasingly greater emphasis on the use of frames to support the hull.

which is described in detail in several treatises, as well as in an increased number of letters and histories. These same sources also describe the way they were organized, how they operated, and how they should be used in combat. While Arab sources are less prolific, enough information survives to give us a good understanding of how these ships evolved during the last two centuries of this epic naval struggle.

CONSTRUCTION

Several Late Roman and Early Byzantine merchant ships (but no Arab vessels) have been excavated in the Mediterranean, and have revealing useful information about their hull construction. All of these merchant vessels were built using 'shell first' construction – that is, each plank was secured to the one below, working up from the keel to produce the 'shell' of the vessel. Light framing was inserted into place once the shape of the hull had been formed. The planks were secured to each other using mortise-and-tenon joints, pegged together using wooden treenails. In a 4th-century-BC vessel excavated off Kyrenia in Cyprus these mortise-and-tenon joints were closely spaced, with gaps of just 7.5cm between them. The planking of later shipwrecks saw increasingly wide spacing between the joints, which suggest a gradually evolving approach to ship construction.

This trend continued throughout the Imperial Roman period, and into the Early Byzantine era. A 4th-century vessel discovered at Yassi Ada off the south-west coat of Turkey had much looser joints than earlier vessels such as the Kyrenia ship, and these were spaced a little over 24cm apart. A 5th-century merchantman excavated off the Île d'Or on the French Riviera had irregular spacings between the joints, of between 10cm and 30cm. The inference is clear – hull design was changing. This trend is mirrored by increased evidence of caulking during the same period. With the Kyrenia

In the collection of the Museo Nazionale di Ravenna is this Late Roman tombstone, dating to the early 3rd century. It shows a Roman shipwright shaping the frame of a *liburna*. As the hull of the galley has already been built, this relief gives us an insight into how a vessel was built using shell-first construction.

ship there was no need to caulk the hull – the hull was held securely by the mortise-and-tenon joints. This evidently wasn't the case by the 4th or 5th centuries.

A 'shell first' hull built from closely spaced mortise-and-tenon joints was extremely strong, but it was also inflexible. If a hull of this kind was hit by a ram then it would almost certainly stave in planking, and spring joints apart. This would probably cause irreparable damage to the target ship's hull, causing it to take on water and sink. However, a more loosely constructed hull – one that placed less emphasis on the planking joints – was less vulnerable. Not only would fewer joints be sprung when the hull was struck, but any caulking would help maintain the watertight integrity of the vessel. More importantly, this looser form of structure led to a greater emphasis on the vessel's wooden frames to hold the hull together. This made the hull more flexible, and also less vulnerable to damage through ramming. Consequently, the effectiveness of the ram diminished as hull-construction techniques evolved.

For the latter part of our period, the written sources are more helpful in gaining an understanding of Byzantine construction techniques. A late-10th-century Byzantine treatise describes how *dromōnes* were built. *Naval Warfare* was written by an anonymous author for Basil Lakapēnos 'the Bastard' (*c*.925–*c*.985), chief administrator (*parakoimōmenos*) of the Empire, 945–85. It also provides us with a useful dictionary of Byzantine maritime terms. A typical *dromōn* was built from the keel (*tropoi*) up, with each longitudinal plank secured using mortise-and-tenon joints. Temporary stringers or braces were used to hold the planking in place, until the hull was built up sufficiently that it could support itself. When the hull timbers had risen as far as the upper futtocks (*stamines*) the frames (*dryochos*) were added to the inside of the hull, and secured in place using either wooden treenails or iron fasteners. So far this was typical of any vessel built using 'shell first' construction. While the anonymous author didn't provide useful shipbuilding information such as the spacing between the mortise-and-tenon joints or the size and thickness of the frames, some of this can be inferred from archaeological evidence. The wreck of a 7th-century Byzantine merchantman, also discovered off Yassi Ada in Turkey, suggests that the joints were small and widely spaced, which meant that the structural support they offered was not significant. Instead, the vessel's frames augmented the strength imparted by the planking, to create a strong yet flexible hull. While this second Yassi Ada vessel was a merchant ship, her hull lines indicate a vessel built for speed, and her steeply curved stem and stern posts resemble those seen in contemporary depictions of later Byzantine *dromōnes*.

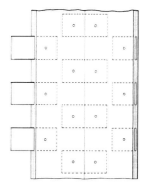

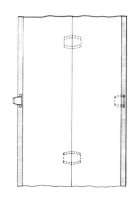

The difference between the mortise-and-tenon construction of the Greek 'Kyrenia ship' of the 4th century BC (above) and that of a Byzantine 'Yassi Ada' vessel of the 7th century AD (below), based on their surviving timbers. Over time the mortise-and-tenon joints become smaller, far less numerous, and more widely spaced. To support this later structure a greater use of internal frames was used, to support the hull.

MOBILITY

Adverse weather had a pronounced effect on galley operation. To preserve the strength of their crews sails were used as much as possible, unless there was no wind, or if battle was imminent. This meant that galleys spent a lot of their sea time under sail, rather than under oars. It was unusual for a galley to be propelled by both oar and sail at the same time. The problem here is that galleys were not really designed as sailing craft. Their long, narrow hulls were ergonomically efficient for oared propulsion, designed to cut through the waves rather than ride over them. This made the vessels poor sailing

A line rendition of a Byzantine *dromōn*, from an original in an illustrated manuscript of the Sermons of St Gregory of Nazianos, compiled in the 12th century. The *dromōn* appears to be of an earlier design, however – possibly 9th or 10th century – and interestingly appears to have her two banks of oars mounted *alla sensile* – in groups of two or three. This is probably anachronistic; it was a rowing system devised in Italy during the 11th or early 12th centuries, and was probably never employed during our period.

craft, as waves tended to break over their bows when under sail, and their shape meant they would have heeled over violently, so that one gunwale would probably be very close to the water. This would have made them uncomfortable sailing craft in anything other than perfect conditions – calm seas with a light breeze. In rough seas they would have little option but to reduce sail or to head inshore for shelter. Even under oars they were poorly designed for operations in rough weather – anything more than a Force 6 meant that the waves were too high and erratic to make propulsion under oars either efficient or viable.

STEERING

These vessels' long, narrow hulls made them fast under oars, but it also meant they would have been difficult to turn. According to *Naval Warfare*, a rudder (*pēdalion*) was shipped over either side of the later *dromōn's* stern quarter, just in front of the captain's cabin – an improvement over the single rudder used in earlier *dromōnes*. The *musattah* was fitted with steering oars on both port and starboard quarters. The steering oar was used to push the water to the left or right, causing the boat to turn in that direction. The more water is pushed – in other words the larger the oar – the faster the vessel will turn. It can also be used to nullify the sideward push of a current, to help keep the vessel on course. Single steering oars were mounted on the starboard side, on the stern quarter of the vessel. The displacement of the vessel meant that turns to port were slightly less efficient than to starboard, as the underwater hull acted to limit the force of the rudder. The solution was to mount two rudders, one on each stern quarter, which greatly improved turning performance. Of course, turning could also be assisted by the angle of the sails if used, or by the action of the oarsmen. While in theory a galley would turn slowly under rudder alone, if one side of oarsmen didn't row while turning, but used their oars as extra rudders, then the vessel would turn very rapidly indeed.

SAILS

A notable characteristic of the *dromōn* was its lateen-rigged sail. The *liburnae* of the Roman navy were fitted with square sails, as Classical Greek and Hellenistic galleys had been. These were conventional rectangular sails, rigged from a single yard on the mainmast. They were practical, but they had their limitations – most notably when sailing close to the wind. A lateen sail is more flexible, as it can be angled to allow the vessel to sail closer into the wind than its square-rigged counterparts. A lateen sail is triangular, and rigged from a diagonally mounted spar suspended from the vessel's mainmast. It has been suggested that the lateen-rigged sail evolved from the square sail between the 1st and the 4th centuries AD (Casson 2014), and that it was first used in small craft in the Aegean basin. However, there is no evidence that this sailing rig was used on Imperial Roman galleys. In fact, what little pictorial evidence there is suggests otherwise.

The first written reference to a lateen sail comes in the 6th century AD, when in the *Life of St Caesarius of Arles* is found a reference to grain-carrying ships called *latenae*. The first naval reference appears in Procopius' account of Belisarius' naval campaign against the Vandals in 532, which mentions how the command ships' sails were

marked: 'The sails of the three ships in which he [Belisarios] and his following were carried he painted red from the upper corner for about a third of the length' (quoted in Pryor & Jeffreys 2006: 153). This reference to an upper corner of these sails suggests these vessels were lateen-rigged. A mosaic dating from the same period in the church of Sant'Apollinare Nuovo in Ravenna, Italy, shows a lateen ship bearing a lateen sail, although the artist depicted it rigged incorrectly, as if the ship were sailing backwards. Then, in the early 6th century the illustrated manuscript *Ilias Ambrosiana* contains a depiction of *dromōnes* which are clearly carrying lateen sails. From the start of the 6th century there are no Mediterranean depictions of square-rigged galleys, although they are seen in images from Northern Europe. While there are precious few depictions of *dromōnes* from the 6th to the 8th centuries, the inference is that from the early 6th century on, these Byzantine warships carried lateen-rigged sails.

While early *dromōnes* were single-masted, a typical large *dromōn* during the era of the Macedonian Dynasty would be fitted with two masts. Both were designed to carry lateen sails. The mainmast was actually shorter than the foremast, as this larger mast was raked forward, so that the two sails didn't become entangled with each other. Each sail was suspended by a yard, fitted diagonally to the mainmast, so that both sailed sloped from bow to stern. Both of the masts were housed in a mast step which rested on the centreline of the vessel, above the keel. Additional support to the masts was provided by standing rigging, attached to the hull. The masts were designed to be removed, by raising them up from the mast steps and laying them parallel to the deck on mast crutches.

The most salient feature found in Egyptian depictions of the *shalandī* from before the 8th century is that like the *dromōn* of that time, it carried a single mast, fitted with a large lateen-rigged sail. Like their Byzantine foes, the *musattahāt* were two-masted, and carried lateen sails. This made them roughly comparable to the new generation of larger *dromōnes* which were now the mainstay of the Byzantine fleet. As with most two-masted, lateen-rigged vessels, the foremast was a little longer than the mainmast, and carried a slightly larger triangular-shaped lateen sail. The iconographic evidence shows that the very tops of the masts were curved forward slightly, reminiscent of the curving end of a hockey stick. This was so that the rope-and-pulley system used to raise and lower the lateen sails operated a little forward of the mast, as the lateen yard or spar appeared to lack the running blocks used in later medieval vessels, along the yard to be hauled up and down the mast itself. Instead, the yard was suspended from the curved mast tip, slightly forward of the mast itself. The masts, too, were angled forward, rather than mounted perpendicularly to the hull, which increased the effectiveness of this form of rig.

OARS

The Justinian Dynasty-era *dromōnes* described by Procopius in the mid-6th century were monoremes – galleys powered by a single bank of oars. Arguably, they would have been smaller than bireme or trireme war galleys, but it is unclear whether the historian meant that all *dromōnes* were monoremes, or that only these single-banked galleys took part in Belisarius' naval campaigns. While bireme *dromōnes* begin to appear in pictorial evidence from the 8th century on, there is no clear evidence to suggest earlier *dromōnes* were anything other than monoremes. The emphasis on speed in the ship name suggests that these galleys were certainly faster than their larger predecessors, and this in turn meant that owing to their small size this speed was achieved by producing a more graceful hull form, rather than by sheer oar power alone. In other words, more muscle power and oars usually means more speed, but not if the smaller vessel was designed to offer less water resistance than a larger galley. The pictorial evidence suggests fast lines, and clearly this was a design characteristic that set the *dromōn* apart from other vessels.

Experimentation with a replica Classical Greek trireme has provided historians with a wealth of information about how galleys were rowed, how much space was required, and how the rowers were arranged. As a result, we can assume that the pivotal points of the two oar banks of a bireme were staggered, so that one set of oars wasn't directly above the other. A spacing (or *interscalmium*) of just over 1m per oar is the minimum space required in order to function, and a gap of 1.5m needs to exist between the lower (*thalamian*) bank of oars and the upper (*thranite*) bank. The upper-deck oars overhung the lower-deck ones, and most probably the oars of the upper bank were longer than those of the lower bank. Approximately two-thirds of the oar extended beyond the oar port, the rest of it being inboard of the hull or bulwark. Typically, this would give an oar span of around 3.5m on either side of the hull.

Naval Warfare provides no dimensions for the stylized, two-masted, bireme *dromōn* it describes, but other sources help us fill in this vital omission. A good starting point is provided by the number of oars and oarsmen carried in these vessels. The *Tactika*, a treatise written on the orders of the Emperor Leo VI 'the Wise' (r. 886–912), states that a typical *dromōn* of around 900 had around 50 oars per side, in two banks. The upper bank of oars might have a few more oars, but probably fewer than 30. A sensible average of 52 oars on each beam might be appropriate, or a total of 104 oars per galley. As each oar would have been pulled by a single oarsman, this equates to 108 rowers. The *Tactika* adds that some *dromōnes* had a crew of 200 oarsmen, of whom 50 would serve the lower banks, and 150 the upper one. This gives an improbable total of three men per oar on the upper deck, which seems highly unlikely. For reasons

This small fragment of a damaged Egyptian wall painting dates from the mid-7th century – the time of the Arab conquest of Egypt. The vessel it depicts is clearly a galley – possibly a bireme one – with a steeply sloping stem post, but little more can be gleaned from the representation. However, it remains a rare fragmentary depiction of the type of galley the Arabs would have built to form their first fleet.

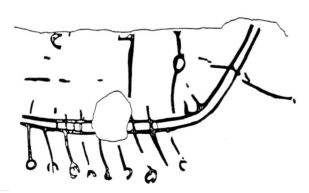

given above, it seems likely that *dromōnes* were powered by one rower per oar – an average of 50 in the upper bank and 50 in the lower one. If any additional oarsmen were carried they would have been used as replacements, or as marines or missile troops, but exactly how this system operated in practice is unclear.

We already know that the basic *shalandī* of the 7th and 8th centuries was very similar to Byzantine *dromōnes* of the period, as the Arabs were able to draw upon shipbuilding expertise in their newly conquered provinces of Egypt and Syria. By the 9th century, however, contemporary writers were able to differentiate between larger Arab *shalandiyyat* (*musattahāt*) and smaller ones (*shawānī*). While some of the latter might have been biremes, the inference is that most if not all of them were single-masted monoremes, like the original Byzantine *dromōnes* upon which their design was based. While *shalandī* oar configurations aren't always shown in surviving illustrations, in most cases these appear to be depicted as a single bank of oars. The inference is that before the 8th century most Arab *shalandiyyat* were monoremes.

A tantalizing glimpse of an Arab *shalandī*, redrawn from a painted and glazed ceramic fragment produced in the Middle East during the 13th century. It now forms part of the collection of the Museum of Islamic Art in Cairo. The bireme galley carries a quilted lateen sail, and a decorated stern post.

The exception, of course, is the *qādis* or *qārib* mentioned earlier, which may well have developed into the larger, more powerful *musattah* of the 9th century. The appearance of the *musattah* is more problematic. While most of the Arab images we have show monoreme galleys – presumably of the smaller *shīnī* type – two images exist which show larger biremes. The pictorial evidence for these *musattahāt* suggests the vessels had a deeper draught than the earlier *shalandiyyat*, but as with the later *dromōnes* the lower tier of oars was enclosed by the upper deck, leaving just the upper tier exposed to enemy fire. The *musattah* carried approximately 25 oars in each bank, for a total of about 100 oars per vessel. The 14th-century Arab treatise by Muhammad ibn Mankali (d. 1382) states that 'the minimum number of thwarts (*zawāghir*) on each [beam] should be fifty, and the men should be above and below' – in other words, in two banks (quoted in Pryor & Jeffreys 2006: 647).

DEFENSIVE STRUCTURES

PROTECTING THE OARSMEN

The description by Procopius stating that 6th-century *dromōnes* were fitted with complete decks sets these craft apart from triremes and *liburnae*. These earlier Byzantine vessels had a half-deck, or more precisely a lateral part-deck (*katastrōma*), which ran along the centreline of the vessel, but which left the rowing benches uncovered. While some *liburnae* might well have had fully covered decks, the inference is that this was an innovation that was particularly associated with the *dromōn*. Procopius gives the primary reason for the decking as protection – it was

A Byzantine *dromōn*, from a graffito found on the wall of the Hephaistion in Athens, dating from some time after the start of the 9th century. This bireme carries a large lateen sail, a spur ram at the bow, and some form of stern cabin, mounted above the sharply curving stern post. Note the heads of the upper bank of oarsmen are visible – those of the lower rank were fully protected by the upper deck.

there to protect the oarsmen from enemy missile fire. This is mirrored in a letter written in the 520s by the Italian politician Cassiodorus (*c.*485–*c.*585) on behalf of Theodoric 'the Great', king of the Ostrogoths (r. 475–526). It described the *dromōn* as a vessel 'carrying a great many oars but carefully concealing the form of the men' – a reference to the deck covering the oarsmen (quoted in Pryor & Jeffreys 2006: 130).

As with other aspects of the later *dromōn*'s design and intended function, *Naval Warfare* casts valuable light on the protection it afforded the crew. According to *Naval Warfare*, above the hull was a deck (*ikria*), which was cambered so it was highest along the centreline, and curved gently downwards towards either beam. Inside this hull structure floor timbers (*enkoilia*) were secured to the frames, to encase the entire enclosed lower deck. Inside this enclosed hold (*kytos*), rowing benches or thwarts were fitted to these floor timbers, and the upper futtocks were pierced with oar ports. This meant that the rowers serving these oars were completely protected from enemy missile fire by the upper deck of the vessel. Above this upper deck a high bulwark (*peritonaion*) ran around the entire upper deck, and again it was pierced with a second row of oar ports on either beam. This meant that the later *dromōn* described by our anonymous author was a bireme, with two banks (*elasiai*) of oars on each side. Shields could be hung from the gunwales of this bulwark, which could be used by the oarsmen if they were required to fight rather than to row. On the outside of the bulwark a box-like structure (*epōtides*) protected the oars where they passed through the oar ports. Pictorial sources suggest the Arab vessels didn't use a protective box covering their oar ports.

FIGHTING PLATFORMS

According to the *Tactika*, a fortified forecastle (*pseudopation*) served as the vessel's main fighting platform in the prow (*prōra*) of the *dromōn*, and protected the crew of the Greek Fire projector (*siphōn*) located directly underneath this forecastle. *Naval Warfare* mentions a second fortified fighting position, forward of the mainmast. Referred to as a wooden castle (*xylokastron*), this is clearly the same structure as that enigmatically described in the *Tactika*: 'They [the crew] will set up the so-called wooden castles … fortified with planks, around the middle of the mast on the largest dromons, from which men will throw into the middle of the enemy ship millstones or heavy iron [weights], like sword-shaped blooms …' (quoted in Pryor & Jeffreys 2006: 229). Further aft, towards the stern, stood a small captain's cabin (*krabatos*), on top of which was a third small fighting platform.

It is evident that the Arabs also built fighting platforms on many of their vessels. In the latter part of our period there are enigmatic Byzantine references to Arab *kastellatoi* – galleys which were fitted with defensive 'castellation' (see Pryor & Jeffreys 2006: 165). These were presumably similar to the 'wooden castles' described in the Byzantine *Naval Warfare* treatise – fighting platforms located either in the bow or amidships, presumably one on each beam, mounted over the upper rowing thwarts. Like the later Byzantine *dromōn*, the *musattah* appears to have had two main fighting positions – in

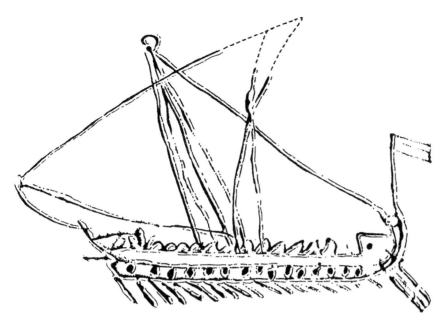

This graffito from Malaga in Spain shows a single-masted Byzantine *dromōn* of the late 7th or early 8th centuries. She appears to be a monoreme, with two steering oars, a narrow spur, and a small fighting platform in her bow. A structure of some kind can also be identified at her stern. Shields appear to line her gunwales, above the single line of oar ports. The original graffito is now in the collection of the Museo Naval, Madrid.

the bow, and amidships, either between the two masts, or around the mainmast. It is unclear whether this amidships fighting platform spanned the whole beam of the ship, or – as with the Byzantine version – it was mounted on either beam, above the amidships rowing benches. In his treatise, Muhammad ibn Mankalī writes: 'In each ship there should be a tower beside the mast, the tower is surrounded by planks all around so that fighting men can stand on them and throw [missiles] towards the middle of the enemy ship' (quoted in Pryor & Jeffreys 2006: 647). This description suggests a single platform, rather than one divided between the two beams, but the exact nature of its dimensions and appearance is unclear.

ARMAMENT

The range of weaponry used by both sides was remarkably similar, with the one significant exception of Greek Fire. Even that weapon had its less effective Arab counterpart in the form of fire pots and incendiary missiles. Then, from the mid-9th century on, the Arabs gained access to this secret technology, and were able to use Greek Fire projectors of their own. The weapons carried reflected the tactical doctrines of the age, where long-range missile fire was used to damage enemy vessels long before contact was made. These were particularly useful when war galleys were called upon to support amphibious landing operations or coastal raids, or during the siege or assault of ports.

If the rival fleets continued to close then short-range missile weapons were used, including Greek Fire projectors, small ballistas and catapults, supported by conventional missile troops such as archers. Again the aim was to disrupt the enemy fleet, crippling vessels rather than destroying them. The two sides would then close within grappling range, and the real battle would begin. Despite the large array of missile weaponry available, naval battles during this period were still decided by hand-to-hand combat, resulting in the capture of enemy ships rather than their destruction.

Byzantine *dromōnes* were armed with an array of weaponry, both projectile weapons and close-combat arms designed for use in a boarding action. The most deadly of these weapons was the 'flame thrower' (*siphōn*, pl. *siphōnes*); such tubes were fitted to the bow of the *dromōn* from which Greek Fire could be projected. These were augmented by a selection of mechanical devices.

SHIP-MOUNTED PROJECTILE WEAPONRY

Most Byzantine *dromōnes* were fitted with anti-personnel ballistas (*ballistrai*) – weapons which used hand-powered torsion to draw large bows, and which loosed iron quarrels known as 'mice' (*mues*) at the enemy. These weapons were usually fitted in the bow, often on a platform above the *siphōnes*, and at the stern. These locations were used because they offered a reasonably clear arc of fire. Other smaller ballistas known as *toxobalistrai* were fitted to the sides of the hull, on the gunwale above the oar decks. Their quarrels were referred to as 'flies' (*muiai*).

GREEK FIRE

In the spring of 672 a large Arab fleet arrived in front of Constantinople, and landed an army that besieged the city. The fleet was still there in the summer of 678, when the Byzantine imperial fleet decided the time was right to attack. This would be no ordinary naval battle. The Byzantines would unleash a new, secret weapon – one that was as fearsome as it was deadly. This new terror weapon was called Greek Fire. 'Infernal fire' weapons weren't new – they had been used in the Mediterranean in various forms since the 5th century BC. What made Greek Fire different was a combination of its combustible qualities, its delivery system and the fact that it could be used at sea against highly combustible warships.

Essentially, Greek Fire was a flammable liquid which was sprayed out of the nozzle of a metal-clad tube called a *siphōn* by the Byzantines. While the invention of the combustible liquid is often credited to Kallinikos of Heliopolis, a Syrian scientist

Probably the most familiar image of a Byzantine *dromōn* in action, and the only contemporary depiction of Greek Fire being used, this manuscript illustration forms part of the *Synopsis historion* of John Skylitzes, *c*.1160. The original manuscript is housed in the Biblioteca Nacional de España in Madrid. Unfortunately while the scene itself is dramatic, it adds little to our understanding of what these weapons looked like, and how they were operated.

ARAB SHIPBOARD CATAPULT, 7TH CENTURY

While the ballista was more commonplace in both Arab and Byzantine fleets, catapults of the kind shown here were also carried. This example is based on Late Persian weapons of the early 7th century, which appear to have been similar to both Arab and Byzantine descriptions of these torsion-powered machines. The treatises suggest that as well as launching rocks at the enemy, other suitable projectiles might include: pots containing Greek Fire or quicklime; spiked iron projectiles wrapped in combustible material, designed to stick against an enemy hull or deck; and bags of small caltrops, designed to prevent the enemy from moving easily around his own deck. One of the more outlandish suggestions in Leo VI's treatise was to fire pots or baskets containing venomous snakes into the crowded deck of an enemy warship.

How these projectile weapons were mounted isn't specified in the Byzantine and Arab treatises. However, to function efficiently they would have required some form of swivel mounting, such as a large stanchion with a socket on top, through which a rod on the underside of the weapon could be slotted. Some form of elevation device would also be required, although whether this was done using quoins or a more elaborate ratchet device is unknown. It has been suggested (Gardiner 1995) that a reinforced boat-shaped frame was used to house Byzantine *ballistrai* and catapults.

These Early Byzantine *dromōnes* are depicted in the *Vergilius Romanus*, a manuscript of the late 5th century housed in the Biblioteca Apostolica Vaticana. Imperial Roman naval *liburnae* were originally fitted with a ram (*embolos*), curving upwards slightly and fitted to the stem post above the waterline, but pictorial evidence suggests this had fallen from favour by the late 5th century. *Liburnae* depicted on Trajan's Column (*c.*AD 114) carry this form of curved ram, as do other Roman galleys depicted in the early 3rd century and the 4th century AD. This illustration shows what appears to be a similar form of curved ram, albeit one without any evident metal tip, but it is actually supported by a chain or coupling, attached to the stem post. A ram wouldn't need any such support, as it was an integral feature of the hull. This suggests that by this period the ram had evolved into a spur. The *Tactika* mentions that a thin spur – which may have been detachable – was attached to the stem post just above the waterline. The spur would have been constructed from wood, but was clad in iron, to reduce the risk of damage when it rode up over the rowing banks of an enemy vessel.

living in Constantinople, its exact origins remain shrouded in mystery. So too are the ingredients used to make it. Current thinking is that it was formed using a combination of naphtha distilled from pools of crude oil found in present-day Azerbaijan, known by the Greeks as 'the land of the naphtha fountains'. This was mixed with equally flammable stabilizing ingredients such as resin or wax, quicklime, sulphur, turpentine or saltpetre, and this was then distilled to create a flammable but stable liquid.

The use of Greek Fire remained a closely guarded secret for just over 150 years. By the early 9th century, however, it seems the Arabs not only discovered the recipe, but were able to duplicate the delivery system as well. The Arabs as well as the Byzantines had used incendiaries throughout this period – weapons such as hand-thrown fire pots (resembling flammable grenades), fire-tipped arrows, and mangonel or catapult-fired incendiary projectiles. However, by 835 both Arab and Byzantine accounts mention the existence of an Arab *harrāqa* – a fire ship, equipped with a Greek Fire projector. It was later claimed by Byzantine historians that Euphemios, *droungarios* of the Sicilian thematic fleet, took the secret with him when he defected to the Arabs in 827. In any case the weapon was in limited use in Arab *harrāqat* in the Syrian, Sicilian and Egyptian fleets by the middle of the 9th century. Now that both sides employed 'infernal fire', the Byzantines had to augment their fire-fighting capabilities on board their warships, and tactically they learned to identify and avoid enemy *harrāqat* if they possibly could.

GREEK FIRE SIPHON, LATER 8TH CENTURY

While no detailed description survives of a Greek Fire system, sufficient references exist to build up a reasonable picture of how these worked. Experimental versions have recently provided us with useful information about their effectiveness. The incendiary liquid was housed in a sealed tank (**1**), which was heated to near boiling point by means of a brazier or furnace box (**2**). It was served by one or two sets of hand-operated bellows (**3**). When the device was ready to be used two crewmen would pump air into the tank by means of a two-handed pump (**4**). An extant force pump of this kind is housed in the Museo Arqueológico Nacional in Madrid. When the pressure was sufficiently high inside the tank a valve (**5**) would be opened, and the liquid would be forced through a tube, which led to the siphon, or spout. Some means of directing this – most likely a simple hand-turning bar (**6**) – allowed the siphon to be aimed. As the liquid jetted out of the nozzle it was ignited by means of a wick lamp (**7**), located just beneath the siphon nozzle (**8**). The 'infernal fire' would then continue on its way towards its target – ideally hitting the decks or sails of an enemy ship.

Experiments have shown that ranges of around 12–15m could be achieved, more than enough to bridge the gap between two galleys closing for battle. Greek Fire burned on everything it touched – ships, men, and even the surface of the sea itself. It is hardly surprising it was dubbed 'infernal fire'. Because of its strategic value and the secrecy surrounding its use, Greek Fire projectors were only fitted to the *dromōnes* of the imperial fleet – the *Karabisianoi*. In the *Tactika* it is claimed that the main *siphōn* in a *dromōn* could sometimes be augmented by two secondary *siphōnes*, mounted on each beam of the ship, but whether these were small hand-held *siphōnes* or more substantial fitments is unclear.

In the 11th-century Byzantine treatise on siege warfare attributed to Hērōn of Byzantium and now housed in the Biblioteca Apostolica Vaticana, this illustration shows how the Byzantines were prepared to use their *dromōnes* as siege platforms by decking pairs of them over to form larger, temporary catamarans. These could then be used to house scaling platforms, battering rams or siege towers. Note the use of what appears to be bronze statuary to weigh down the wooden platform spanning the two pairs of *dromōnes*.

CLOSE-COMBAT WEAPONRY

During the early part of our period both Byzantine and Arab galleys had stem and stern posts that curved upwards, but none of the Arab vessels appears to have been fitted with a spur. Conversely, the spur (*peronē*) was an important feature of the early *dromōn*. The developments in hull-construction techniques described above led to the gradual replacement of the ram with a spur. It had a completely different function. Its job was to ride up over the oars and hull of the enemy ship, smashing the oars as it did so. Once the enemy ship was rendered immobile it could be finished off at leisure by marines or missile troops. Several references are made to this tactic, and an illustration from a work by the chronicler John Skylitzes (c.1040–after 1101), *Synopsis historion*, shows Byzantine *dromōnes* riding over the hull sides of Rus' ships during a 10th-century engagement in the Bosporus. A Latin word for the spur was *calcare* (from the verb meaning 'to trample'), which underlined its naval function.

The move from a ram to a spur probably took place gradually, at some stage between the 1st and the 5th centuries AD – in other words during the Imperial Roman period. It therefore coincided with the evolution of the *dromōn*, and the two were clearly linked. A galley fitted with a ram needed to have a heavily timbered bow, but without it bow shapes could become trimmer and more elegant. This coincides with the introduction of raked stem and stern posts, and this may also be linked to the association between the *dromōn* and speed. This evolution was complete by the start of the 6th century, when the *dromōnes* of the Early Byzantine navy were first making their mark in the Mediterranean.

An even more spectacular weapon was the 'crane' (*geranion*), designed to destroy ships which came alongside the Byzantine vessel. It was fitted to the centreline of the *dromōn*, and consisted of a large upright wooden post, surmounted by a wooden arm which projected out from it at right angles, like a hangman's gallows. The Byzantines referred to it as looking like the upper case of the Greek letter *gamma* (Γ). The upright post could be pivoted using ropes, and the arm swung out over the side of the *dromōn*. Once it lay over an enemy ship, containers of flaming pitch could be dropped onto the enemy decks, or poured out from a container which was operated by a pulley system (*manganon*). This would have involved some kind of hinged cauldron, although the exact design of it is unknown. These same pivoting cranes or *gerania* could also be used to operate grappling hooks or ladders fitted with hooks, to facilitate boarding, or to attack the walls of an enemy port. These naval siege weapons could be augmented by similar contraptions designed to extend boarding platforms out over the enemy walls. The *gerania* were sometimes referred to as *keloneia*, from the Greek word *kelon*, meaning a pivoted swinging beam.

RECONSTRUCTING THE DIMENSIONS

From the spacing per oarsman outlined above, and comparing the size and appearance of *dromōnes* in contemporary iconographic evidence, we can determine that the large, late-9th-century *dromōn* described in *Naval Warfare* was approximately 28.6m long at the waterline, and 31.25m long overall. Its beam at the waterline was approximately 3.5m, while its beam at the level of its upper deck was around 4.4m. By extrapolating information from mid-12th-century Byzantine sources, we can assume that for a vessel of this size the lateen yards would be just over 14m long for the foremast, and 13.1m for the mainmast. This means that the tip of the foremast would have been around 21m above the waterline (Pryor & Jeffreys 2006: 248).

Interestingly, even after leaving 1.2m on each side of the hold for the *thalamian* oars, that still leaves a space of just over a metre amidships. This would have been occupied by a central walkway, or when required it could have been used to house stores or supplies or even animals. However, this central space was also needed by the crew themselves, and so it seems more than likely that any stores were stowed beneath the rowing thwarts, rather than along the centreline of the vessel. Accounts survive of *dromōnes* and *shalandiyyat* being used as amphibious craft during this period, and some carried horses. It has even been suggested that horses could fit in the hold in this central walkway on large *dromōnes*, with just enough headroom for the animal to stand upright. Quite what the oarsmen thought of this temporary arrangement is unrecorded.

What is striking about the later Arab craft is their hull shape. They appear to have been deeper-draughted than earlier vessels, presumably so they could carry a larger crew of oarsmen and marines. Their stem and stern posts were both rounded, giving them – at least in profile – the silhouette of a contemporary merchant vessel. The difference, of course, was that these were oared warships, rather than merchant galleys or sailing vessels.

41

Bireme *dromōnes*, from the *Synopsis historion* by John Skylitzes, housed in the Biblioteca Nacional de España, Madrid. This stylized depiction of Byzantine *dromōnes* shows them with twin stern post structures, typical of the latter end of our period, and small spurs at the bow.

Therefore their beam was dictated by the mechanics of oar power. This meant a high ratio of length to beam – anything from 8:1 to 10:1 being optimal. The narrower the beam, the easier it became to propel the galley through the water. Given an average spacing of around 1m per oar, this made the rowing deck of these vessels around 25m long.

Additional space was required both in the bow and the stern. The *musattah*'s bow contained a fighting platform or open deck area, used by soldiers and missile troops, while deck space in the stern was required to house the helmsmen's positions beside the steering oars, the stern cabin used by the *musattah* commander, and additional space for marines. It has therefore been estimated that a typical *musattah* of this period would be around 35–40m long. Given the ideal ratios quoted above, a beam of around 4–5m could be expected, although some maritime historians have suggested this could be as wide as 6m, giving a length-to-breadth ratio of approximately 6:1. This, though, would have placed these vessels at a disadvantage to their Byzantine foes, as the additional water resistance this wider beam gave the vessels would have made them slower and less manoeuvrable. A more likely solution is that like the later Byzantine *dromōnes*, Arab galleys of the period had outward-sloping hull sides, so that the hull widened between the waterline and the upper deck, where the upper banks of oarsmen were located. Not only would this make these galleys better rowing platforms, as it reduced the risk of interference between the two oar banks, but it would also provide additional deck space for the marines and upper-bank oarsmen, without dramatically reducing the ergonomic efficiency of the vessel.

THE COMBATANTS

HIGHER ORGANIZATION AND COMMAND

BYZANTINE

For both military and administrative purposes the empire was divided into districts, each known as a *thema* (pl. *themata*). Each *thema* was controlled by a *stratēgos* (pl. *stratēgoi*), who held both civil and military authority in the region. The *stratēgos* was responsible for raising troops in his *thema*, and in coastal areas for maintaining a fleet of *dromōnes*. These thematic fleets made up the bulk of the Byzantine navy. They were supported by an imperial fleet, based on Constantinople, known as the *Karabisianoi*, the first fleet of the empire. Its term derived from the Greek word *karabion* ('ship'), and literally means 'people of the sea'. In the later 7th and 8th centuries the principal thematic fleets were those of the *Kibyrrhaiōtai* (based in the Gulf of Antalya in Asia Minor, and then Samos), the Aegean (based in Pyraeus), the Sicilian (primarily based in Syracuse), the African (based in Carthage) and the Italian (based in Ravenna). The loss of both of these last two cities led to the disbandment of their thematic fleets. Just as their thematic *stratēgoi* did, these thematic *droungarioi* enjoyed a substantial degree of operational freedom, both to expand and maintain their fleet, and to protect their territorial waters. Of all the thematic fleets, those of the *Kibyrrhaiōtai* and the Aegean remained the most important in the East, and their Sicilian counterpart served as the bedrock of Byzantine maritime power in the West, at least until the fall of most of the island to the Arabs.

This thematic system worked particularly well as a means of providing a timely local response to Arab incursions. If the local thematic fleet was unable to cope with an Arab threat, then reinforcements would be summoned from neighbouring *themata*, and from the *Karabisianoi*. It had its disadvantages too – the independence given to thematic *stratēgoi* led to occasional rebellions against imperial rule. During the 9th century the loss of Sicily and Crete led to the decline in importance of the Sicilian fleet, and a corresponding increase in that of its Aegean counterpart. A new thematic fleet was also created to counter the new threat from Crete, and was based on the island of Samos. Similarly, a detachment of the *Karabisianoi* was now stationed at Mytilene on the island of Lesbos, from where it could respond more quickly to Cretan incursions into the Aegean than it could from Constantinople. This situation continued until 960, when Crete was recaptured. At that point the thematic fleets of the Aegean were combined, and moved to new bases on the reconquered island.

Further to the east the *Kibyrrhaiōtai* continued to protect the empire from attack by both the Syrian and Egyptian Arab fleets, and gradually they forced the Arabs from their small forward bases along the southern coast of Cilicia. The recapture of Cyprus in 965 provided the Byzantine navy with a new forward base, where it was well placed for attacks on the Syrian fleet based at Tarsus. A reduced Sicilian thematic fleet continued to operate from bases in southern Italy, although effectively it was reduced to little more than a coastal defence force. If a Byzantine fleet needed to operate in the Central Mediterranean, elements of the *Karabisianoi* and possibly the Aegean thematic fleet were dispatched there, where they joined forces with the rump of the Sicilian fleet in limited operations.

ARAB

The Arab arrangement of forces appears to have been essentially similar under the Umayyads and their Fātimid successors, with powerful regional fleets based in Syria, Egypt and – after 700 – in North Africa. However, the caliphs never seem to have adopted a standing force similar to the Byzantine imperial fleet. Partly, this is the result of geography; the Arab capitals (Damascus, Baghdad, Kairouan, south of Tunis, and Cairo) were inland, or well up-river, and so did not require a home fleet to guard them, although there was a small flotilla stationed at the mouth of the Nile to protect its approaches. Another factor was the political structure of the caliphates, with strong centrifugal tendencies, both religious and political, encouraging the development of regionally independent sub-dynasties, which maintained their own navies. There are strong indications that in the first two centuries of Muslim naval activity, ships and fleets were often more piratical than naval in character, and only after administrative structures grew up and matured was there a definitive move towards more professional standing navies. By the 9th century in some areas such as Fātimid North Africa – and certainly by the 10th century in many places – Arab fleets were more closely modelled on the Byzantine navy, with ships built and maintained in government arsenals and commanded by professional officers.

In Moorish Iberia, the admiral in command of the fleet was one of the great officials of the realm. Still, throughout the period of Islamic expansion, pirates and corsairs – privately sponsored, but whose income could be taxed – were numerous, and could be employed to ravage shipping and harass coastlines ahead of the more permanent invasions. Newly conquered coastal territories rapidly became forward bases for pirate fleets raiding further into the economic core of the Byzantine Empire. Both Crete and Sicily became home to large raiding forces that harried shipping and coastal settlements

on a regular basis, and the annexation of much of the southern coast of Asia Minor allowed the development of the port of Tarsus as a base for the powerful Syrian fleet. After the conquest of Iberia, the ports of the Mediterranean coast became home to the Moorish fleet, and served as a staging point, first for the plundering, and later for the capture of the Balearic Islands and coastal Provence.

The Emperor Leo VI 'the Wise', whose treatise on naval warfare provides us with a wealth of information on the organization, operation and tactical doctrines of the Byzantine fleet. A copy of his treatise *Tactika* was captured by the Arabs, translated, and then reproduced together with Arab amendments and annotations by Muhammad ibn Mankalī.

OFFICERS AND CREWS

BYZANTINE

Each individual *dromōn* was commanded by its captain (*kentarches*, pl. *kentarchoi*), the term equating to the commander of an *ousia*, a crewing detachment of around 100 men. In battle the *kentarches* would take up his station in the bow, where he had the

45

BYZANTINE COMMANDERS

For most of this period the commander of the imperial fleet always outranked the thematic fleet commanders. This overall imperial commander, whether he commanded thematic ships, his own fleet or a mixture of the two, was referred to as the *stratēgos* or the *droungarios tou ploïmou*, the commander of the imperial fleet. (He was also referred to as the *basilikon ploïmon*.) Beneath him came the commanders of the various thematic fleets, who each held the rank of *droungarios* (pl. *droungarioi*). Sometimes the terms *tourmarchēs* (pl. *tourmarchai*) or *droungarios* were used to refer to lesser admirals – effectively the commanders of divisions within the thematic or *Karabisianoi* fleets. In the *Tactika* it is written that in the past the governors of maritime *themata* had borne the title of *droungarios*, but that in Leo VI's reign they had become *stratēgoi*, and that lesser *tourmarchai* and *droungarioi* now served under them. While the titles may have changed with time, the basic command structure within the fleet remained largely unaltered.

As the fleet's commander-in-chief the *stratēgos* was responsible for its strategic deployment as well as its battle deployment, and the choice of tactics. He – or rather his administrative staff – also held responsibility for the logistical needs of the fleet, and made sure the ships were properly equipped, provisioned, crewed and ready for battle. His subordinate *droungarioi* advised him through the aegis of a war council, and of course they held their own subordinate commands, controlling their own thematic component of the larger fleet. The *stratēgos* commanded a division or 'battle' of galleys, while his subordinate *droungarioi* commanded the other divisions that made up the fleet. Each of them would have a suitably imposing flagship. In fact the *Tactika* advises commanders to use a large, fast *dromōn* such as a *pamphylos* (an over-crewed, large *dromōn*) as their command vessel, and to crew it with hand-picked men (*pamphyloi*). Below the *droungarioi* were the squadron commanders, each known as an *archon* (pl. *archontes*) and commanding a squadron of 3–6 galleys, leading them from his own squadron flagship. The same advice on the selection of a divisional or squadron flagship and crew was also offered to the *droungarioi* and *archontes*.

The most striking feature of both Arab and Byzantine senior commanders was the way they combined their naval responsibilities with political or military ones. Several Byzantine emperors took direct control of their combined imperial and thematic fleets – not always with success. For instance, Constans II led his fleet into action at the Battle of the Masts, but appeared to lack the ability to co-ordinate the actions of his fleet. As a result he attacked piecemeal, and was soundly defeated by Abdullāh ibn Sa'ad ibn Abī as-Sarh. His successor, Constantine IV, elected to direct the naval battle fought off Constantinople in 678 from the city walls, rather than from the deck of his flagship. This made perfect sense – he was better placed to co-ordinate his fleet's actions from that better vantage point. In the early 8th century the Emperor Anastasios (r. 713–15) led a fleet against the Arabs, while Leo III 'the Isaurian' also used Constantine's vantage point on the city walls while directing the Byzantine counter-attack off Constantinople in 718. The 10th-century emperors Romanos I Lakapenos and Constantine VII 'Porphyrogennetos' are also known to have taken direct command of their fleets when they felt circumstances required it.

Several less exalted Byzantine naval commanders rose to prominence during this period, and varied in their ability to co-ordinate powerful fleets. For example, the *stratēgos* John the Patrician proved incapable of defeating the Arabs off Carthage, so his second-in-command, Tiberios Apsimaros killed him and took over the command. He went on to seize the imperial throne, becoming the Emperor Tiberios III (r. 698–705). Both these commanders led troops on land as well as their fleets. This duality of land and sea commands was typical of this period. Other Byzantine naval commanders were notable for less salubrious reasons. Euphemios, a Sicilian naval commander, defected to the Arabs in 827, while Constantine Gongyles (*fl*.913–49) and the *patrikios* (governor or high-ranking official) Malakenos were both defeated by the Arabs in the mid-10th century, off Crete and Calabria respectively. In both these latter cases these commanders were attempting to co-ordinate a campaign fought both on land and sea, and simply weren't up to the challenge.

ARAB COMMANDERS

In Arab fleets, the title of the fleet commander wasn't as rigidly fixed as it was in the Byzantine navy. The term *almilland* ('admiral') was commonly used, but there was no clear form of differentiating between ranks. Instead, titles were awarded for specific missions. For instance, the commander of a Moorish amphibious expedition was referred to as the *amir al-rahl*. Islam's first naval hero was Abdullāh ibn Sa'ad ibn Abī as-Sarh, the victor of the Battle of the Masts. Like most commanders of the period he combined political and naval responsibilities – at the time of the battle he was also the governor of Egypt. It was his task to raise an Egyptian fleet, and in 645 he used it to thwart a Byzantine attack on Alexandria. Although he was a self-taught naval commander he rose to the challenge, and his performance in 655 was exemplary. His superior at the time was Mu'āwiyah ibn Abī Sufyān, who had fought in the land battle of Yarmouk, and then as governor of Syria he

built a fleet there, which he used to launch a raid on Cyprus in 648. It was he who masterminded the larger naval and military campaign that resulted in the victory of 655. His skill in balancing military, naval, diplomatic and political matters resulted in his seizure of the caliphate in 661.

These two gifted founders of the Arab navy were followed by others of a similar vein, albeit without Caliph Mu'āwiyah's rare abilities. Most notable were Hasān ibn an-Nu'umān al-Ghasānī and Abū Hafs Umar al-Ballūtī. The former was the conqueror of Byzantine Africa, who masterminded the naval defence of Carthage in 698. The latter was essentially a privateer, whose opportunistic seizure of Crete led to the island becoming a centre for Arab privateering for more than a century. Like the privateering leader Leo of Tripoli, al-Ghasānī and Abū Hafs campaigned both on land as well as at sea, further demonstrating the need for versatility and a range of talents among the very best Arab commanders.

This well-known medieval Middle Eastern depiction of Arab commanders, musicians and standard bearers is one of the few images to show us what Arab flags and banners might have looked like during this period. While we know that Arab *shalandiyyat* carried flags, and a few banners are depicted in contemporary representations of these vessels, we have no clear notion of their appearance, and are forced to assume that they would have been similar in appearance to these later banners.

Byzantine *dromōnes*, as depicted in the 11th-century manuscript *Synopsis historion*. While the vessels themselves are only depicted in the most cursory and stylistic way, the Byzantine troops crewing them are shown wearing the impressive scaled armour and helms that would have been worn by the marines who crewed such vessels. While the manuscript was produced much later, this scene attempts to recapture the events – and the armour – of the 9th century.

best view of the action. The *kentarches* was assisted by a number of officers, the most senior of whom was the first officer (*prōtokarabos*, pl. *prōtokaraboi*). Confusingly, the *Tactika* equates the term to that of the helmsman, a statement supported by other accounts, who describe the helmsman as *prōtokarabos*. Therefore the exact nature of the *dromōn*'s command structure remains unclear. Another senior officer was the bow officer (*prōreus*), who commanded the marines of the bow fighting platform and Greek Fire projector. The keeper of the standard (*phlamoulon*) may have been some form of signaller, but the term also equates to a Classical Greek term referring to the master of the oars, who regulated the time of the oarsmen and transmitted the captain's orders. Undoubtedly he had a deputy who performed a similar function on the lower deck, but this necessary position is unrecorded. A *dromōn*'s rowers were probably led by a first oarsman (*protelatai*), while the two bow oarsmen on the upper deck were given additional responsibilities, suggesting they held the equivalent of a modern petty officer's rank. One of these was designated the siphon commander (*siphōnarios*, pl. *siphōnarioi*), while his fellow bow oarsman was responsible for supervising the anchors.

In Leo VI's *Tactika* and *Peri thalassomachias*, a work written in about 1000 by the Byzantine commander and statesman Nikēphoros Ouranos (*fl.c.*980–*c.*1010), a total of around 100 oars and 100 oarsmen was considered common on a medium-sized bireme *dromōn*. This correlates to the numerous clerical references to *ousiai*, a unit of oarsmen equivalent to the complement needed to crew a *dromōn*. An *ousia* was regarded as comprising 108 to 110 men, which equates to the crewing level mentioned in the two treatises mentioned above. These men were primarily oarsmen, but could also function as lightly armed marines or missile troops. Some *ousiai* are described as being *pamphyloi* ('hand-picked'). Together, the oarsmen (*kōpēlatai*, sing. *kōpēlatēs*) and marines – *stratiotai* (sing. *stratiotēs*, meaning 'soldier') or *polemistai* (sing. *polemistēs*, meaning 'warrior') – formed the *ousia*, the administrative unit referring to oarsmen, but which effectively became a crewing unit, incorporating officers – *archēgoi* (sing. *archēgos*) or *hēgemonoi* (sing. *hēgemonos*) – as well as oarsmen and marines. Clearly there was some degree of flexibility between the various roles, as upper-deck oarsmen were expected to participate in the fighting during a boarding action, and were issued with shields, light armour and weapons. However, the marines would bear the brunt of any fighting. The *Tactika* advocates that *kentarchoi* pick their crew carefully, selecting the bravest and strongest of their oarsmen to serve on the upper deck. The less courageous should be sent to the lower oar deck, where they would form a reserve if required.

Unfortunately, this neat correlation between oars, crew numbers and the *ousia* isn't as simple as it looks. In documents relating to the Byzantine expedition to reconquer Crete in 949 there are references to 20 *dromōnes*, each carrying two *ousiai*. Both the *Tactika* and Ouranos also state that on the largest *dromōnes* there should be 200 men on board, 50 of whom operate the *thalamian* oars. Clearly the remaining 150 men cannot all be oarsmen, so the inference is that 100 of them are dedicated marines or missile troops. This reinforces the statement already made in the *Tactika* that the oarsmen of a *dromōn* could also function as soldiers.

Another crewing description of the Cretan expedition mentions a large *dromōn* having a crew of 300 men, 70 of whom are marines. This equates very roughly to three *ousiai*. Clearly, 230 of these men couldn't all be oarsmen – it was ergonomically impossible to operate a *dromōn* with more than one man per oar. Even if these large *dromōnes* had a significantly larger number of oars, there would be still far more oarsmen than oars. The only sensible solution is that while the 70 men mentioned as marines were specifically trained, armoured and equipped, the remainder could either serve as oarsmen or as lightly armed marines, as the situation dictated. This means that the vessel could have as many as 200 marines on board, 70 of whom were dedicated soldiers.

Obviously, the exact size of a ship's complement would be tailored to the needs of the vessel, and to the tactical requirements of the specific expedition or mission. The limiting factors were weight and space. An extra 100 men carried on board a *dromōn* could increase its displaced weight by as much as 10 tonnes. Given the light construction of these vessels and their size, this would make it ride up to 15cm lower in the water. That in turn would have a significant impact on the vessel's speed,

This very interesting depiction of a Byzantine *dromōn* from the *Synopsis historion* by John Skylitzes is stylized, but it clearly shows a vessel with pronounced twin curves at bow and stern, a single bank of oars, and a very small spur at the bow. Note the Byzantine banner flying from the vessel.

handling and ability to operate in rough, open water. In anything other than light sea and wind conditions the lower bank of oars would have been rendered unworkable, necessitating the shipping of the oars and the sealing of the oar ports.

The other problem was one of space. Given that a large *dromōn* of this period was around 28.6m long and 4.4m wide on its upper-deck level, and given that much of this deck space would be taken up by the *thranite* oars and rowers, a central walkway space of just over 2m would be left. The small deck areas at the bow and stern tapered off, save for the fighting platform in the bow. This means there was probably less than 50 square metres of deck space available for the marines and missile troops to operate in. This space was constricted even further by the presence of masts, hatches and the stern cabin. It is hard to see how 100 fighting men could be accommodated in such a small space, let alone how they would be able to fight.

The inference is that where large crews of two or three *ousiai* are mentioned, then these extra men were probably carried for a specific operation, or were being transported on board, rather than all of them serving as soldiers. The vessel would be crewed by around 100 oarsmen, who could also double up as lightly armed marines when required, but additional men could be embarked if the operational situation dictated it.

ARAB

In a *shalandī*, the captain (*ra'īs*) commanded the vessel, and was responsible for seamanship, shipboard routines, the oarsmen and navigation. He was assisted by one and possibly two subordinates, who freed him of all responsibility for the overseeing of the crew (*nawātiya*, corresponding to the Greek word *nauta*), and for leading the ship in battle. The crew were therefore commanded by a first officer, the *qā'id al-nawātiya* ('Master of the Sailors'). This division of responsibilities stemmed from the early years of the Arab Conquest, when a crew would be recruited from a pool of Syrian or Coptic Egyptian mariners, who were unused to naval discipline, and to fighting. Effectively they were civilians, pressed into naval service. The *qā'id* took direct control of the oarsmen, but on smaller *shalandiyyat* it appears that he also commanded the marines. This responsibility included the direction of the ship in battle. On larger warships it is highly probable – but not recorded – that another *qā'id* took over command of the marines, and supervised their tactical employment, along with that of the ship itself. Again, in the early years of Arab nautical endeavour, marines were drafted directly from the ranks of the army, hence the need for a division of administrative and practical responsibilities.

It was claimed by the 14th-century Arab author Muhammad ibn Mankalī that by the late 8th century the Arabs had adopted a more Byzantine approach to the appointment of senior positions on board the *shalandiyyat*. Muhammad ibn Mankalī provides us with a few hints of this, in its few references to Arab shipboard organization. He states that 'in each ship there should be a shipwright' – a senior carpenter whose task was to supervise the repair of the vessel, and what today would be called 'damage control'. The captain was to be in the bow (*quddam*) of the vessel, and 'each ship should have four individuals trained specifically for looking after the injured, and to take off their weapons, and to give them food and drink' (quoted in Pryor & Jeffreys 2006: 646). Presumably a similar level of medical support was available in Byzantine *dromōnes*, as it is also advocated in the *Tactika*. Finally, the Arab translation of Leo VI's treatise declared that 'two officers are needed in charge' of the oar decks, one for each level.

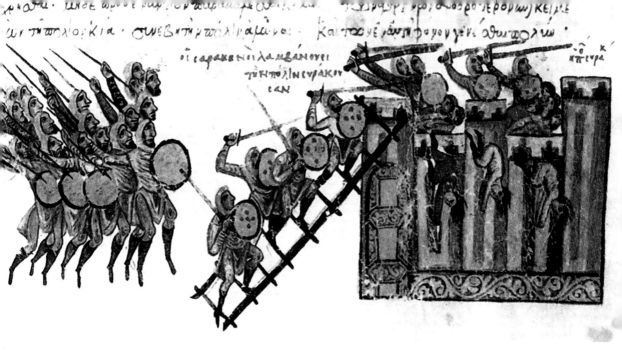

In his *Al-adilla al-rasmiyya fī l-taʿābī al-harbiyya* ('Official Instructions for Military Mobilization') Muhammad ibn Mankalī included a section entitled *Nukat fī qitāl al-bahr* ('Remarks on Sea Warfare'). In it he described the crewing arrangements on board *shalandiyyat*. After discussing the number of oars, he added that there should be 'two men for each thwart, half of them to be oarsmen, and they are those of the lower level, the other half to be the fighters and they are those of the upper level' (quoted in Pryor & Jeffreys 2006: 248). This passage is confusing, as the author based it on a translation of a Byzantine naval manual written by Leo VI. However confusing the phrasing, it suggests that a *shalandī* of this period was crewed by a similar number of oarsmen and marines.

This draws on a tradition that in Egypt a crew of a warship served as oarsmen or as marines. The two tasks weren't interchangeable. Oarsmen were not warriors, and weren't expected to fight as such, except in dire circumstances. Instead, professional marines were embarked to act in this capacity, either as missile troops, the crew of heavy weapons such as catapults or naphtha throwers, or as melee troops. The parity of numbers suggested by Muhammad ibn Mankalī indicates that Arab galleys were well provided for in terms of marines – probably more so than in the *dromōnes* of the Byzantine fleet. By contrast, on Byzantine *dromōnes*, while there was a distinction between marines and oarsmen, the latter were lightly armed, and were expected to play their part in any boarding action if the need arose. Effectively, one side had more specialist marines on board their ships, while the other had a more flexible manning system.

Muhammad ibn Mankalī also informs us that on Arab *shalandiyyat* the captain (*raʾīs*) would take up station in the bow before battle was joined. This suggests that his command position was on the bow platform, where he would have a relatively unimpeded view of the sea around his vessel. In that position he would also be better placed to see signals made by the senior officers of the fleet. Interestingly, the same Arab treatise mentions that a typical *shalandī* would have a crew of 200 men, including troops 'for throwing' (missile troops) as well as 'fighters' (marines armed for hand-to-hand combat). This equates to the crewing levels mentioned above, in the two *ousiai* embarked on Byzantine *dromōnes* during the Cretan expedition of 949.

Arab troops storming the defences of Palermo, in the 12th-century depiction of these 9th-century events offered by John Skylitzes' *Synopsis historion*. The establishment of an Arab presence in Sicily allowed Arab *shalandiyyat* to raid deep into the Adriatic and Tyrrhenian seas. The appearance of these soldiers would be typical of that of the marines embarked on Arab galleys of the period.

COMBAT

While there are several contemporary treatises that outline the theories and tactical doctrines of naval combat, actual accounts of naval battles during this period tend to be disappointingly brief. Both Byzantine and Arab historians tended to avoid lengthy descriptions of engagements, and focussed more on the general sweep of campaigns, or the exploits of key commanders. They also weren't naval experts, and so the accuracy of any description of naval combat needs to be weighed against what we know about tactics and weaponry. That is exactly where we begin by looking at the theory of naval warfare during this period, before moving on to its practice.

THE THEORY OF COMBAT

TACTICAL MANUALS

A number of Byzantine tactical manuals offer advice to fleet commanders, covering a range of topics, from advice on waging naval campaigns to what tactics to adopt when fighting a sea battle. The most significant of these treatises was the *Tactika*, attributed to the Emperor Leo VI 'the Wise'. It was produced around 900, at a time when the Byzantine Empire was under intense pressure from the Arabs, particularly those in Sicily and Crete. Of its twenty chapters or 'constitutions' (*diataxeis*), only one offers advice on naval warfare, but it provides us with a valuable source of information on Byzantine tactical thinking. It presumably drew on more than two centuries of Byzantine naval experience, and so it almost certainly represents the current naval doctrines of the time. However, as it was also written when the Byzantine navy was on the defensive, it contains numerous elements which reflect this particular situation, such as the importance of

S.CATERINA

husbanding naval resources, preserving the fleet and of avoiding battle if at all possible. As such it lacks many of the references to the more aggressive tactics that had served the Byzantine fleet well in other periods of its long history. It recommends only giving battle at favourable odds, and in advantageous circumstances. However, it also proposes that when battle was joined, then all of the naval resources at the disposal of the fleet commander should be harnessed to ensure victory.

Almost as influential was the *Peri thalassomachias* treatise of Nikēphoros Ouranos, written around 1000. In it, Ouranos – an experienced Byzantine commander – updated Leo VI's *Tactika*, and the later *Praecepta militaria* of the Emperor Nikephoros II Phokas (r. 963–69) as well as other earlier treatises, and then explored some new recommendations for the deployment of a Byzantine fleet. Again, it probably drew on many tactical ideas that had been developed long before the manual was written, and so it reflected current tactical thinking by the Byzantine navy. *Naumachia* ('Naval Battle'), a tactical treatise written in the mid-10th century and attributed by some scholars to Syrianos Magistros, acts as a useful bridge between these two better-known works. Taken together, these three treatises provide us with a detailed insight into how the Byzantine fleet operated. Arab tactics largely mirrored those of their Byzantine opponents. Leo VI's *Tactika* was translated into Arabic, and formed the core of the treatise by Muhammad ibn Mankalī, first published in the 14th century.

Both Byzantine *dromōnes* and Arab *shalandiyyat* were frequently used to transport and land troops, both infantry and cavalry. This 16th-century depiction of Turkish galleys shows how this was done – the galleys were simply run bow-first onto the shore, and the troops disembarked from them as if they were modern military landing craft.

53

PREPARING FOR BATTLE

The *Tactika* places great emphasis on professionalism. Commanders are told to ensure that the crews of their ships were fully trained, and that the fleet was well-versed in the naval manoeuvres that would give it an edge over its Arab opponents. The fleet commander is also advised to seek accurate intelligence about the enemy's location, intentions, size and fleet composition, and to use scouting vessels to keep track of enemy movements. The fleet commander is expected to know the geography of the chosen battle arena, and to use it to his advantage. For instance, if the fight was going to take place off an enemy-held coast, then he is advised to fight close inshore, to encourage the enemy to abandon their galleys for the safety of the shore if they are hard pressed. Before battle is joined, the commander is advised to hold a council of war, so that all his senior officers know what his plans are, and what is expected of them. Individual initiative is subordinated to the need to work together as a well-drilled naval machine. A signalling system is laid down, so that the individual squadrons and ships of the fleet could be kept informed; tactical plans are recommended, and it is recommended that the carrying out of them should be fully rehearsed before battle commences.

In the treatise *Kitāb al-Kharāj* (Book of Revenues), written for the fifth Abbasid caliph, Hārūn al-Rashīd (r. 786–809), the duties of the Arab fleet commander are outlined in a set of special instructions, advising him on the way to manage his fleet, how to select commanders, how best to allocate crewmen, and what he needed to do to maintain the combat effectiveness of his fleet. Muhammad ibn Mankalī added a rewriting of Leo VI's instructions when issuing advice to an Arab fleet commander: 'If the situation becomes stressful, you, O commander, should be the first to display perseverance and fortitude; and keep your person from actual combat when you meet the enemy in battle, unless it becomes absolutely necessary. Rather you should confine yourself to commanding and making decisions' (quoted in Pryor & Jeffreys 2006: 666). One decision that was independent of the senior *almilland* was the selection of his marines, who were supplied by a land-based commander. In his 'Remarks on Sea Warfare', Muhammad ibn Mankalī advised that: 'No bribe should be taken from any

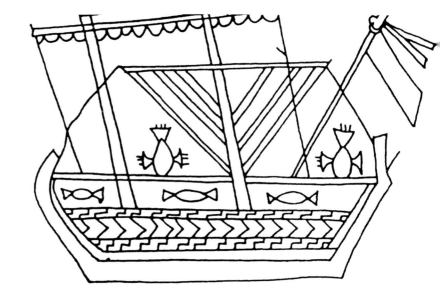

The Arab response to Greek Fire was the *harrāqa* ('fire-ship'), which wasn't an incendiary vessel; rather it was a *shalandī* equipped with 'infernal fire' weapons such as fire pots and naphtha projectiles. Once the Arabs learned the secret of Greek Fire these galleys were adapted to carry Arab-built Greek Fire projectors. This image is taken from an Arab manuscript of the late 13th century attributed to the explosives pioneer al-Hasan al-Rammah (d. 1295).

soldier; selecting warriors is a condition and prerogative of the commander (*za'īm*) of the army …' (quoted in Pryor & Jeffreys 2006: 649).

FORMATIONS AND FLEET TACTICS

Given the opportunity, experienced Byzantine fleets could assemble for battle in a variety of ways, depending on the situation they faced. The *Tactika* makes this clear:

> Sometimes [you should draw up] a crescent-shaped or sigma-shaped formation in a semi-circle, with the rest of the dromons placed on one side and the other [i.e., of the flagship] like horns or hands and making sure that the stronger and larger [ships] are placed on the tip … The crescent arrangement should be such that, as the enemy attack, they are enclosed within the curve … Sometimes it [the fleet] should be divided into several formations, either two or three according to the number of dromons under you. When one formation has attacked, the other falls on the enemy either at the rear or from the flank when they are already engaged, and with these reinforcements attacking them then the enemy breaks off fighting. (Quoted in Pryor & Jeffreys 2006: 505)

The Byzantines evidently viewed the adoption and maintenance of the most appropriate battle formation to be a crucial element of success. Every effort was to be made to maximize the effectiveness of the fleet and limit the degree to which the *dromōnes* could inadvertently impede one another's fighting potential. According to the *Naumachia*:

> When about to engage in naval warfare, we should arrange the stronger and more heavily crewed of the ships alongside each other and place them in front of the rest. Each should be far enough away from the next so as to prevent their obstructing each other during the conflict and their colliding with each other, and the equipment of the soldiers aboard should be better than that of the rest … The remaining ships should follow behind, drawn up like those in front but not haphazardly.
>
> We should keep the formation not only during the conflict itself but should preserve it satisfactorily also during the manoeuvring before the arrival of the enemy, since this is what we also do in infantry warfare. The reason for this is to enable the expedition which has become used to its good battle formation to maintain it during a crisis. (Quoted in Pryor & Jeffreys 2006: 463–65)

The Arabs also placed great value upon the adoption of the most appropriate battle formation, depending in part upon the relative strengths of the two fleets about to fight one another. According to Muhammad ibn Mankalī:

> The first thing I should inform you of in this regard is that you should know when it is appropriate to surround your enemy in a half circle formation. And you should enjoin the captains of the ships to line up for you, as a right wing and left wing …
>
> At another time, you should approach them [the Byzantines] with light fast ships (*mashshāya*), and then these should pretend to flee. Once the enemy ships disperse to pursue what they have seen, you should attack them using your other ships, and when the enemy's fighters are worn out you can send your rested companions against them. If you can, you should avoid the enemy's large ships and target the weak ones. If your

OVERLEAF The engagement shown here was fought off the Ionian Islands in 880, and pitted a small Byzantine thematic fleet supported by 45 *Karabisianoi dromōnes* against an Arab raiding force from Sicily. The two forces encountered each other unexpectedly in straits between Kerkyra (Corfu) and the Greek mainland. Both sides arrayed for battle, but neither was willing to risk attacking the other. In the end the two fleets separated, only for the Byzantines to launch a rare night attack which destroyed the Aghlabid fleet. In our view of the stand-off the Byzantines have deployed in a crescent formation, supported by a reserve, while the Arabs have formed up in four successive lines, with the heavier vessels in front. The Arab flagship (**1**) is located in the centre of the front line, as is that of his Byzantine counterpart (**2**). In the Arab fleet, secondary warship lines (**3**) are deployed behind the vanguard. These wings or secondary lines are commanded by Arab and Byzantine (**4**) squadron commanders, in their own flagships. Both sides have halted just outside extreme missile range, and are about to lower their masts as these would be a liability once battle had commenced. Those vessels carrying heavy missile weapons have been deployed in the rival front ranks, where the Arab (**5**) and Byzantine (**6**) ballista crews will have a clear field of fire when the two fleets close to within range.

fleet is large you should meet the enemy with some of the ships and let the others rest. Once the enemy is tired of fighting and your men are tired also, you can replace them with the rested ones. (Quoted in Pryor & Jeffreys 2006: 662–64)

While such tactics were equally appropriate for either side, given the heavy reliance by the Arabs on privateers – particularly the fleets based in Crete, Sicily, Moorish Iberia and Tarsus – the adoption of this feigned-flight tactic must have been particularly appealing to some Arab commanders. Similarly, the privateering elements in a larger Arab fleet might have been less willing to adopt the solid defensive tactics employed by the Byzantines, and instead to use more aggressive tactics. The notion of holding part of the fleet in reserve appears to have been employed in a number of sea battles during the latter part of the period – such as Thasos (829), Milazzo (888) and Tyre (998) – with the Arabs letting the enemy expend their missiles and relying on the higher and stouter sides of their *shalandiyyat* to fend off boarding attacks. When the time was right the rest of the Arab fleet would make its move, closing with the weakened enemy to deliver a decisive counter-attack. Whatever tactics were employed, though, once battle was joined it was usually up to the courage, skill and fighting abilities of the individual galley crews to determine who would emerge the victor.

CLOSE-QUARTERS COMBAT

In the naval clashes of the Ancient World, victory was achieved by sinking enemy warships. Before the beginning of our period this had changed – victory was now determined by boarding and capturing enemy galleys. This was due to the demise of the ram, and the increasing strength of warship hulls as pure shell-first construction gave way to the increasing use of frames to strengthen the hull. This basic premise – that battles were fought at close range, and were won by melee – would remain the key element of Mediterranean galley warfare until the 16th century and beyond. That weaponry capable of destroying ships existed didn't alter this basic concept. While the use of Greek Fire might prove decisive, and lead to the destruction of numerous enemy ships, it remained an adjunct to the main doctrine of naval warfare, just as the use of artillery in the Late Medieval period and the Renaissance was never more than a way of damaging and demoralizing the enemy before battle commenced.

Before a galley went into battle, it was wise to lower the masts. In both the *dromōn* and the *shalandī* the masts could be unshipped from the mast step located just above the keel, and the foot of the mast was lifted up to the height of the upper deck. It was then carefully lowered onto mast crutches located on the centreline of the vessel, most probably forward of the foremast or aft of the mainmast. This was possible because the masts were relatively thin and light. The importance of this is clear – if the vessel went into battle with its masts up they would make the galley particularly vulnerable from fire attacks, or the oarsmen and marines would have to risk having masts, yards, sails and rigging falling on them. Accounts of galleys that failed to step their masts before battle show that this was seen to be an invitation for disaster.

The clash of galleys was preceded by the firing of missiles, and the squirting of Greek Fire. Large ballistas could loose bolts which could travel for up to 450m, although effective combat range was perhaps half that. Ship-mounted catapults had a range of around 300m when firing stones, or about 200m when firing fire pots.

Extreme bow range was arguably about 200m, with effective range about half that. When vessels came within hand-fired missile range then both Byzantine and Arab warships relied on missile troops to weaken the enemy before the two ships ranged alongside each other and a boarding action would begin. There is some debate about whether or not the Byzantines had hand-held crossbows before the start of the 11th century. It is possible the *cheirotoxobolistrai* mentioned in 10th-century Byzantine records were hand-held crossbows, but Anna Komnene (1083–1153), daughter of the Emperor Alexios I Komnenos (r. 1081–1118), claimed that in the late 11th century such weapons were unknown in Byzantium. They may have fallen from favour by then, or more likely an earlier Byzantine crossbow (known as the *tzangra*) was considered less powerful than its Western counterpart, and so its use was abandoned in favour of more powerful deck-mounted ballistas. The Byzantines also relied on more conventional archers and javelinmen, though, and these were deployed in a platform at the bow of the ship, over the *siphōnes*, at the stern, and possibly amidships as well. The Arabs also used large numbers of archers, and their projectiles included fire arrows as well as conventional ones. The Greek Fire projectors that equipped Byzantine *dromōnes* (and Arab *harrāqat*) had an effective range of around 12–15m. Small darts and javelins were designed to be thrown at short ranges of less than 10m, while rocks or fire pots hurled onto enemy decks would have required the two vessels to be alongside each other.

When the missiles had been expended, the two sides closed and grappled. Iron grappling rods are listed in Byzantine inventories for the Cretan expeditions of 911 and 949. Leo VI's *Tactika* tells how pikes (*menaula*) would be thrust through the enemy oar ports, or poles used to fend off approaching enemy galleys. Sometimes attacks were carried out by pairs of ships, one on either side of the enemy vessel, or sometimes a pair of galleys would be roped together, to create a single fighting platform. That way the crew of several ships could fight together as a cohesive force, and men could be sent to where they were needed most, rather than remaining on

In this mosaic from the Late Roman temple at Hadrumetum (now Susa in Tunisia), a Roman *liburna* of the 3rd century is shown with its mast lowered, and supported on a mast crutch. In ideal circumstances, later Arab and Byzantine galleys would also lower their masts just before they went into combat, to reduce the risk of fire from incendiary weapons.

their own vessel. Whatever the preliminaries might be, a naval battle usually degenerated into a brutal period of hand-to-hand combat.

Byzantine treatises of the late 9th and early 10th centuries explain just how the Byzantines prepared for this, stating that a properly equipped *dromōn* should contain a large contingent of soldiers, including the oarsmen, who were all trained marine infantrymen. Among the *kataphraktoi* who were stationed on the upper deck, everyone from the *kentarches* down to the last man on the upper deck should be extensively protected by armour, whether mail corslets, lamellar cuirasses or padded felt jackets. Both missile troops and melee troops were protected in this way, although the former tended to wear the lighter padded armour rather than metal protection. Shields were carried, or in the case of the unarmoured or lightly armoured oarsmen they could be unhooked from the bulwark before a boarding action began. Other protection consisted of helmets, and for the heavier *kataphraktoi* greaves and vambraces might also have been worn. The Arabs placed a greater emphasis on mobility, although well-armoured marines were used to spearhead the attack, or to form the core of a ship's defence.

As for individual close-combat weaponry, swords, spears or pikes and axes were carried by both Byzantine and Arab marines and seamen. Smaller axes were used to cut grappling lines or the rigging of enemy ships, while each combatant would also have used whatever personal weapons he could wield, such as knives, wooden staves and scimitars. Given the restricted nature of a boarding action, those troops who possessed full armour would have been at a considerable advantage in a shipboard melee, not just because of their protection, but also because such troops were usually highly trained in close-combat fighting. No amount of battle experience, though, could guarantee victory in a naval combat where flammable projectiles and unquenchable fire were commonplace.

Byzantine *dromōnes* attacking a fleet of Rus' galleys in the Black Sea, as shown in the *Synopsis historion* by John Skylitzes, produced around 1160. This provides us with the best indication of how the spur was used to ride over the oars and sides of enemy galleys. The original manuscript is housed in the Biblioteca Nacional de España, Madrid.

BATTLE HISTORY

To illustrate a little of the tactics used by both sides, we need to look at a selection of naval encounters for which more than a cursory account of the engagement has survived. It is important to remember, however, that set-piece battles were only one facet of a fluid and evolving conflict that often involved raiding, sieges and outright piracy across the length and breadth of the Mediterranean.

THE BATTLE OF THE MASTS, 655

The Battle of the Masts was fought off the port of Phoenicus (now Finike) on the Lycian coast – now Ankyra province in modern Turkey. Despite both ibn Abd al-Hakam and the Byzantine chronicler Theophanes the Confessor describing the battle (making it one of the most documented naval engagements of the period), details are disappointingly sparse. The battle took place between the Arab fleet of Abdullāh ibn Sa'ad ibn Abī as-Sarh and a larger Byzantine naval force led by the Emperor Constans II. The Arab fleet

Byzantine *dromōnes* carrying troops, pictured coming to the relief of Abydos, a small Byzantine port on the Dardanelles, which was besieged by rebel forces in 821–23 during the revolt of Thomas the Slav. Image from John Skylitzes' *Synopsis historion*, dating from the mid-11th century and now housed in the Biblioteca Nacional de España, Madrid.

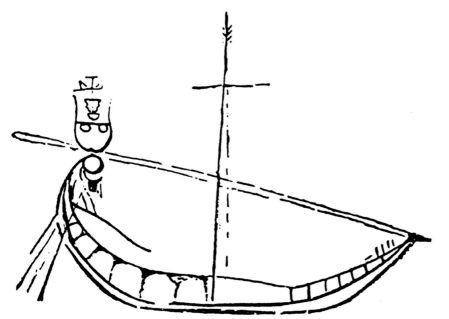

This 6th-century graffito from an Egyptian temple shows a single-masted vessel, probably a warship, fitted with a lateen sail, and a single small yard for a square sail above it. This is another example of local shipbuilding traditions being adapted for Byzantine and later Arab use in the Middle East. The figure in the stern – if it is a figure – probably represents a helmsman.

61

A two-masted vessel carrying lateen sails, taken from a wall painting in Kellia in Egypt, produced during the early 7th century. It therefore represents a vessel – whether a galley or a pure sailing craft is unclear – of the time of the Arab conquest of Egypt.

consisted of approximately 200 *shalandiyyat*, while the Emperor commanded around 500 *dromōnes*. The Arab chronicler ibn Abd al-Hakam (803–71) claimed the Byzantines had as many as 1,000 ships, but this isn't borne out by Byzantine records – a total of around 500 Byzantine warships is more accurate. He also stated that half of the Arab crews were ashore when the battle began. Being so heavily outnumbered, the Arabs withdrew into the confined waters of Phoenicus Bay, and tied their ships together, to create a vast floating raft. Before battle was joined the Emperor ordered that banners be raised, showing the sign of the cross, and the Arabs responded by displaying the crescent, and banners containing inscriptions from the Quran. The flagships of both sides flew images of cross and crescent at their mastheads – hence the name of the battle.

The fight began with an exchange of missiles – ibn Abd al-Hakam mentions the use of bows and arrows, and Theophanes mentions the hurling of stones. The Byzantine fleet then launched several direct attacks against the naval fortress of *shalandiyyat*, resulting in hand-to-hand fighting. Presumably both sides had lowered their masts before the melee began – this was standard practice during the period unless one fleet was trying to outmanoeuvre the other or the battle had begun unexpectedly. The Byzantines – according to Theophanes – were woefully unprepared for the battle, and the sea was soon full of Byzantine blood. Losses were heavy on both sides, but not all of the Byzantine warships could attack the enemy at once, and so their superiority in numbers was nullified. Eventually, the Byzantines gave up the attack, at which point ibn Abd al-Hakam claims that ibn Sa'ad ordered the Arab *shalandiyyat* to cut themselves loose and give chase.

Theophanes added that the Emperor was almost captured as the Arabs grappled his flagship, and he threw off his imperial robes and dived over the side. He was rescued by one of the sons of Buccinator – a Byzantine commander known as Qanatir to the Arabs who may have been a Slavic prince – but his rescuer was killed as the emperor was spirited to safety. In his study of the battle, one modern historian wrote that: 'The most rudimentary rules of naval warfare were grossly neglected by both parties, partly because of the Byzantines' underestimation of their enemy. The two fleets faced each other the whole night before their engagement without any plan … None of the parties took into consideration the wind' (Christides 2002: 90). This is a little harsh – ibn Sa'ad seems to have come up with a very clear plan, and was rewarded with the Arabs' first naval victory in the Mediterranean.

THE BATTLES OFF CONSTANTINOPLE, 717–18

Unfortunately, other naval battles of the period are only given a brief mention in contemporary sources. One exception is the Arab attack on Constantinople in 716–18. This was the second Arab attempt on the city. In 671 a large Arab invasion fleet led by Caliph Mu'āwiyah had entered the Aegean, and wintered there. The following spring it passed through the Sea of Marmara, and landed troops outside the walls of Constantinople. The Byzantine capital was besieged, and the Arab fleet continued to lie off the city for six years, leaving only to go into winter quarters. Eventually, though, in 678 this Arab fleet was defeated in battle off Constantinople, thanks to the first-ever use of Greek Fire by the Byzantine navy. The Arab defeat was so complete that Mu'āwiyah had been forced to sign a 30-year truce with the Emperor Constantine IV (r. 668–85).

While the Arab sources for the second Arab attack on the Byzantine capital are very scant, Theophanes the Confessor provides us with our main account of events. In the spring of 717 the Arabs besieged Constantinople for a second time, their fleet of 1,800 galleys and transports being deployed in support of an enormous army which it had ferried across the Bosporus. An Arab alliance with the Bulgars posed an additional threat to the Byzantines, until the Emperor Leo III 'the Isaurian' (r. 717–41) persuaded the Bulgars to ally with him instead. The Byzantines sent in *dromōnes* equipped with Greek Fire. The action was directed by the Emperor himself, watching the battle from the walls of Constantinople. Theophanes claimed: 'Some of them, still burning, smashed into the sea wall, while others sank in the deep men and all, and others, flaming furiously, went as far off course as the islands of Oxeia and Plateia …' (Theophanes 1982: 88–89).

After the conflagration of the 717 battle, the Arabs kept their naval forces at arm's length, wary of the Byzantines' fire weapons. The siege dragged on during an especially harsh winter, until the spring of 718, when the Byzantines attacked again, guided by Egyptian Coptic deserters who disliked their Muslim overlords. This time Theophanes

OVERLEAF The Arabs had first experienced Greek Fire at the climax of their first siege of Constantinople in 678, when their fleet was scattered and destroyed thanks to this Byzantine secret weapon. In 717 the Arabs returned with an even larger force, and the Byzantine capital was besieged again. Once again it was the Byzantine fleet that finally lifted the siege, thanks to another assault by the *Karabisianoi*, who once again used ships armed with Greek Fire to spearhead their attack. In this plate a Byzantine *dromōn* can be seen squirting its Greek Fire siphon at an Arab *shalandī*. Accounts of men, ships and sails being engulfed in flame imply that the Arabs at least had their masts raised at the time of the attack, which suggests they were taken by surprise. For that reason the Byzantine *dromōn* is also shown with its sail rigged, to help increase the speed of her attack. The siphon and its crew are protected by the bow fighting platform, from where Byzantine missile troops loose their projectiles at the enemy vessel, while marines stand in readiness to lead a boarding attack if required. The *dromōn* commander commanded the ship from this platform, where he had the best view of the action.

Constantinople under attack, from a 10th-century mural. The city walls are defended by soldiers, including archers and supported by what appears to be a pair of Greek Fire siphons, which are directed at the approaching Arab vessel. Cauldrons, presumably filled with boiling oil or pitch, can also be seen being hurled from the battlements.

provides only a brusque statement, saying how the Arab fleet was all but destroyed by the use of Greek Fire: 'the enemy was sunk on the spot' (quoted in Kennedy 2007: 332). The siege was lifted, and the Arab fleet withdrew; a storm finished off what remained of the Arab armada, and the survivors returned to Egypt. Leo III launched a naval counter-attack which reclaimed much of the Aegean basin for the Byzantines. It would take the caliphs three decades to recover from this second disastrous attempt at Constantinople.

THE STRUGGLE FOR CRETE, 824–28

Following its decisive defeat of a combined Egyptian and Syrian fleet off Cyprus in 747 the Byzantine navy remained the dominant naval force in the Mediterranean, despite its lack of naval mastery in the Western Mediterranean, and the growing naval power of the Italian city-states. In the West the Frankish fleets based in what is now Catalonia effectively neutralized the naval power of the Iberian Arabs – the Moors – while in the East the recovery of new Abbasid caliphs lacked the enthusiasm their Umayyad predecessors had shown for naval power. The reign of the Emperor Michael II 'the Amorian' was wracked by revolt, however, and the *Kibyrrhaiōtai* –the Byzantine fleets based in Asia Minor – offered their support to the rebel, Thomas the Slav

(*c*.760–823). Although the central imperial fleet was able to crush this revolt, the Byzantine navy was seriously weakened.

This distraction allowed the Arab leader Abū Hafs Umar al-Ballūtī (d. *c*.855) to establish a foothold in Crete between 824 and 828. Over the next four decades, three Byzantine attempts to evict the Arabs were unsuccessful, and the Arabs were eventually able to expand their control over the whole island. While many of the details of this campaign are unclear, it is generally assumed that the Arabs advanced westwards, towards Chandax and Souda Bay. This dramatically altered the strategic situation. From the port of Chandax on Crete's northern coast the Arabs now had a base they could use to launch raids throughout the Aegean, and from which to sever Byzantine sea links with Rhodes and Cyprus to the east, and Sicily and Italy to the west. In 829 the Arabs defeated a Byzantine fleet off the Aegean island of Thasos. The Cretan Arabs' temporary naval supremacy in the Southern Aegean that resulted would undermine the ability of the Byzantines' Aegean-based fleet to limit the scope of these Arab incursions.

THE DAMIETTA RAID, 853

Finally, an engagement that wasn't a naval battle per se provides us with a useful account of Byzantine marines in action. In 853 a Byzantine fleet of 100 *dromōnes* captured the Egyptian port of Damietta, and raided the Nile Delta. The attack was timed to coincide with the end of the feast of Ramadan, so a good portion of the garrison was away celebrating in the regional capital. Each *dromōn* carried 150 marines, and this force of 1,500 troops seized the port, burned the mosques, looted

ABOVE In this illustration from the *Synopsis historion* we see a Byzantine force laying siege to the Arab-held enclave of Chandax – now Iraklion – on the northern coast of Crete, during a Byzantine attempt to drive the Arabs from the island in 829. A fleet of *dromōnes* lies at anchor off the port – note their twin curved stem posts, and the spurs fitted to their bows.

BELOW Arab *shalandiyyat*, pictured in the illustrated 11th-century manuscript *Synopsis historion* written by John Skylitzes. In this scene, Arab marines are boarding the vessels, in one of a number of illustrations depicting the Arab invasion of Crete in 824. These very stylized vessels appear to be *dromōnes*, with twin decorative stern posts, a feature associated with the era in which the manuscript was produced rather than that of the events it purports to depict.

PREVIOUS PAGES In 824 an Arab force of Andalusian exiles landed on the south coast of Crete, and began a conquest of the island. Under the leadership of Abū Hafs Umar al-Ballūtī these Arabs gradually drove the Byzantines from much of the island, until by 828 the last Byzantine garrison was overrun. This scene is set during the latter stages of the campaign, where Abū Hafs used his expanding privateering fleet to bypass Byzantine armies, landing behind them, and so driving them back along the northern coast of the island. In this scene Abū Hafs and his officers grouped in his flagship are directing the landing of Arab troops on the coast, where the local Byzantine garrison is offering what resistance it can. Troop-carrying *shalandiyyat* are being followed inshore by small sailing vessels carrying more men, horses and supplies. To the west a small Byzantine squadron has appeared, and Abū Hafs watches anxiously as a portion of his galley fleet is dispatched to intercept the Byzantines.

what they could and made off with 600 captives. At nearby Ushtum they burned the barracks, and destroyed a stockpile of siege engines before leaving for home. No Arab warships were in the area, so the Byzantines were able to escape without being intercepted. During this attack the Byzantine advance guard was heavily armoured, and they and their attendant missile troops easily repulsed what remained of the garrison. Then the more lightly armoured rowers were used to seize the town. The Byzantines returned the following year, and again in 859.

Frustratingly, these tantalizing glimpses are all we have to explain how these warships and their crews fared in action. However, it is enough to build up a picture of naval warfare in this period. The advantage the Byzantine fleet enjoyed through its use of Greek Fire was clearly a battle-winning weapon, but we have no solid information about how these weapons were used in combat. Presumably the siphon crews simply squirted their 'infernal fire' at any Arab vessel within range. Then the *dromōnes* could close in and finish off the demoralized remnants of the fleet, if they hadn't fled already. Commanders had to be flexible, and they and their men needed to react to circumstances, as did Abdullāh ibn Sa'ad in 655. This was made easier by the training and logistical support each side enjoyed, factors which also helped when it came to actual missile exchanges or hand-to-hand combat. Skill, professionalism and training were the real guarantors of victory – these factors and the secret weapon of 'infernal fire'.

ANALYSIS

In the Duel series, this section is usually devoted to qualitative comments on the two protagonists, backed up by statistics and analytical lists of results. Unfortunately, this kind of information isn't readily available for either Byzantine *dromōnes* or Arab *shalandiyyat*, particularly as their naval duel spanned the best part of four centuries. What we can do, though, is to examine some of the more technical aspects of their performance, based on a combination of archaeological and historical study. We can then see how this performance and the very design of the ships themselves affected these two vessels' ability to carry out the strategic and tactical tasks required of them during our period.

This very stylized *dromōn* comes from a 12th-century Byzantine illustrated manuscript, the Sermons of St Gregory of Nazianos, and is in the Greek monastery of Panteleimon, on Mount Athos. While it adds little to our understanding of the *dromōn*, it is worth noting the way the helmsman operates the steering oar, using a small tiller handle rather than by grasping the body of the oar. This illustration also provides us with a useful depiction of the stern decoration of a small monoreme *dromōn*.

This graffito of a single-masted vessel was carved on a roof tile on the Aegean island of Thasos. While it is difficult to date, stylistically the ship appears to date from the Early Byzantine period, possibly around the 6th or 7th centuries. It is unclear whether the hatching along the hull indicates oars, or simply a form of decoration.

SIZE AND SPEED

First, it is worth looking at some of the more general limitations of these vessels. As galleys, their size was limited by the number of oars and oarsmen they carried. As most war galleys of the early part of our period had around 50 oars and oarsmen apiece, in a single tier, this means the vessel's oar deck had to be around 25m long, as roughly 1m per oarsman was needed for the rowers to work. When bireme galleys were introduced, the length of the vessel didn't alter significantly, as one tier of oarsmen was banked above the other, for a total of around 100 oars per vessel. This meant that given space for bow and stern areas, most Arab and Byzantine galleys throughout this period were around 30–35m in overall length. Any larger and the extra weight and displacement would dramatically reduce their efficiency under oars.

Speed through the water is difficult to determine, but given what we know from a reconstruction of a classic Greek trireme, and studies of rowing efficiency, we can estimate that a typical galley of the period had a top speed of around 8–10 knots (15–19km/h). That rate wasn't sustainable, however, and studies of sustainable speed with the reconstructed trireme *Olympias* has shown that after two hours the speed drops below 8 knots (15km/h), and this slows down further over a period of ten hours. Current and wind would influence speed under oar as much as under sail, but it is more likely that a speed of 6–7 knots (11–13km/h) was commonplace, with a maximum speed of up to 10 knots (19km/h) in short bursts of less than an hour. For voyages under sail we have surviving accounts of Byzantine voyages upon which to draw, which suggest a top speed of 7–10 knots (13–19km/h) under favourable conditions, with an average speed of around 3–4 knots (5–8km/h).

RANGE AND LOGISTICS

The other major limiting factor with galleys of this – or any – period was range. Galleys only had a limited storage capacity, and the large crews they carried meant that water stocks were limited. It was estimated that a passenger or soldier on a galley needed 4 litres of water a day, but for each oarsman double that quantity was required. This was particularly true for the oarsmen housed below decks, where poor ventilation added to the demand. So, a Byzantine *ousia* of 108 men would require a minimum of 864 litres per day. When non-rowing supernumeraries such as officers were added this total would be closer to 1,000 litres, or 1 tonne. Water in both Arab and Byzantine ships of this period was stored in amphorae (*kados*), with a typical capacity of around 26 litres apiece. That means a consumption of 38 *kados* per day, per *ousia*. Some *dromōnes* had more than twice that number of crew, which would double the water consumption. It has been estimated that a *dromōn* could sensibly store around 100 *kados* on board.

This meant that a small, one-*ousia dromōn* would have to replenish her water stocks every 2½ days. Larger vessels would have to put into port virtually every day, or else reduce the water ration to below the level needed to keep the crew working at peak efficiency. This effectively meant that galley fleets were tied to the coastline, and their range was limited by the need to find bays where fresh water could be found. The refilling of the *kados* would have taken up precious daylight hours, which reduced the effective range even further. This is why the easiest way to block an enemy galley fleet was to garrison the coast, effectively sealing off all the watering places. While extra water could be carried on accompanying supply ships, this entailed a large logistical effort, and this was only usually an option during large-scale operations.

The very size of a fleet could cause even greater problems. The accompanying table detailing the size of the Byzantine fleet during an attempted invasion of Crete in the early 10th century shows that a fleet of 177 *dromōnes* of various sizes was

Composition of the Byzantine fleet during the invasion of Crete, 911*

The imperial fleet (*Karabisianoi*)

60 *dromōnes*, each having 230 oarsmen and 70 marines – in all, 18,000 men.

40 *pamphyloi*, of which 20 have 160 men each, and the other 20 with 130 men each, plus 700 Rus' mercenaries – in all, 5,800 men (6,500 counting the Rus').

The *thema Kibyrrhaiotōn*

15 *dromōnes*, each having 230 oarsmen and 70 marines – in all, 4,500 men.

16 *pamphyloi*, six having 160 men each, and the other ten with 130 men each – in all, 2,260 men.

The Samos *thema*

Ten *dromōnes*, each having 230 oarsmen and 70 marines – in all, 3,000 men.

12 *pamphyloi*, four having 160 men each, and the other eight with 130 men each – in all, 1,680 men.

The Aegean (Aigaion Pelagos) *thema*

Seven *dromōnes*, each having 230 oarsmen and 70 marines – in all, 2,100 men.

Seven *pamphyloi*, three having 160 men each, and the other four with 130 men each – in all, 1,000 men.

The Hellas *thema*

Ten *dromōnes*, each having 230 oarsmen and 70 marines – in all, 3,000 men.

The Mardaites Army with officers, 4,087, and as auxiliaries another 1,000.**

Summary

The Byzantine fleet consisted of 102 *dromōnes* and 75 *pamphyloi* – a total of 177 vessels.

34,200 oarsmen, 7,140 marines, 700 Rus', 5,087 Mardaites – a total of 47,127 men.

* Information taken from the inventories drawn up in 911 on behalf of the Emperor Constantine VII 'Porphyrogennetos'.

** The Mardaites hailed from the mountains of central Asia Minor; they had a long tradition of serving as mercenary marines with the Byzantine navy. The record didn't state how the Mardaites were embarked.

crewed by 41,340 men, not counting embarked mercenary and auxiliary soldiers. Putting in to a bay every night would have been impractical for a force of this size, as the whole process of anchoring would have taken hours of planning and execution. It was much easier to use supply boats to ferry water to the galleys. Anything else would have been impractical. However, the crew themselves needed to rest, as the oarsmen couldn't maintain a steady speed without it. So, even if watering problems were overcome, the need to remain close to shore remained an operational necessity.

One final note concerns ammunition. While we have a rough idea of the ranges of the various weapons available to the ships' captains, the sources don't address the problem of sustainable fire. Once again, we find answers in the Byzantine records of the Cretan expeditions of 911 and 949. The records for 911 tell us that a typical *dromōn* – carrying 300 men, of whom 230 were oarsmen and/or marines, and the other 70 cavalry soldiers or non-Byzantine auxiliaries – would have carried vast quantities of arrows, which suggests typical fighting range was expected to be within effective bow range, if not closer. This extract from the 949 records shows how these men were equipped.

A pair of *dromōnes* in action against each other – a not infrequent occurrence during a period laced by Byzantine revolts, coups and insurrections. Note the presence of musicians in both vessels. This 11th-century manuscript illustration is from the *Kynegetika*, attributed to Pseudo-Oppian and now housed in the Biblioteca Nazionale Marciana, Venice.

List for the arming of a _dromōn_, from the Byzantine expedition to Crete, 949

50 'Roman' bows with double strings

20 _cheirotoxobolistrai_ (hand-spanned crossbows) with _navklai_ (spanning tools)

10,000 arrows

200 'mice'/'flies' (bolts for ballistas)

10,000 caltrops

Four grapnels with chains

20 stave sickles (for cutting rigging)

100 long spears

100 javelins or short spears

80 corseques (trident-headed staff weapons)

100 swords

70 sewn shields

30 'Lydian shields'

This *dromōn* from the *Synopsis historion* is either an incredibly stylized impression of a 9th-century Byzantine galley, or more likely it depicts a small oared craft of the kind used as a tender by galleys of this period. Vessels of this kind could be towed behind the galley, and were used to ferry men and stores between ships and the shore.

SUMMARY

Taken in total, both the Arab *shalandī* and the Byzantine *dromōn* were highly efficient fighting machines, and very evenly matched. While the Byzantine vessels were almost certainly generally lighter and singly faster than their Arab counterparts, the Muslim warships were purpose-built to be effective fighting platforms. Both *dromōn* and *shalandī*, though, shared the same limitations of speed under oar or sail, or range and storage capacity, and vulnerability to rough weather. Several fleets were destroyed by storms during this period, which shows that while fleet commanders understood these limitations, they sometimes decided to risk everything in order to achieve their objective. This was probably foolhardy – the war galley of this period was a fast, effective but vulnerable fighting machine, whose crew served as both the powerhouse and fighting capacity of their vessel, but also placed limitations on its use. It was a wise naval commander who understood these advantages and limitations, and used them to get the best out of his ships and men.

AFTERMATH

The decline of Byzantine and Arab naval power in the 11th century was marked, and not surprisingly the process began in the Central and Western Mediterranean, where the Italian city-states had been expanding their power. In 1004 Venetian galleys had destroyed a large Sicilian Arab fleet off Bari, on the Italian coast of the Southern Adriatic. In the following year the Pisans crushed what remained of the Arab fleet based in Sicily. This created a power vacuum in the region which the Italians were quick to fill. The sinking of the Tunisia-based Maghreb fleet in a storm off Pantelleria, Sicily in 1052 marked the end of large-scale Arab naval enterprises in the Mediterranean. Three decades later, a Genoese and Pisan fleet would capture Tunis

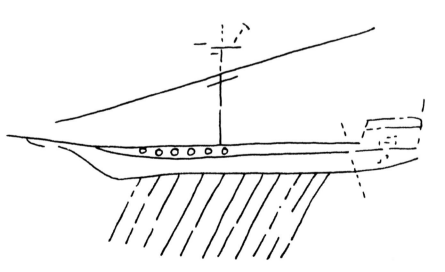

This 13th-century Byzantine galley, from a graffito in the Monastery of St Luke of Stiris near Aspra Spitia in Greece, shows a later form of Byzantine galley, when the lines of the *dromōn* had been amalgamated with those of the Latin *galea* to produce this new form of galley. A lateen-rigged monoreme, it appears lean and fast, albeit with a substantial structure in its stern.

77

In contrast to the images of Byzantine *dromōnes*, this illustration from the *De rebus siculis carmen* of Peter of Eboli, dating from the early 13th century, shows a Sicilian galley operated by the island's new Norman masters. The vessel is a *galea*, the galley type that eventually replaced both the *dromōn* and the *shalandī* during the late 11th century. The manuscript is housed in the Burgerbibliothek, Bern.

and hold it to ransom. This more than anything else underlined just how far the Arab star had fallen during the 11th century.

The Arab maritime decline was matched by a similar ebbing of Byzantine naval power. In the Adriatic, Venice emerged as a major player. Having consolidated her hold on the Northern Adriatic, her fleets moved south, cutting Byzantine supply lines between Greece and Italy, and eventually neutralizing what remained of Byzantine naval power in the region. The Byzantines still had their moments – in 1043 they would defeat a major Rus' naval force in the Bosporus, and the *dromōnes* would successfully defend Cyprus from the Seljuk Turks – but this was nothing when set against the shrinking borders of the Byzantine Empire. For the Greeks, the land defeat at the battle of Manzikert (1071) in Asia Minor at the hands of the Seljuk Turks represented the end of the old Byzantine Empire. What replaced it was a mere shadow of what it had once been.

It was clear that by the mid-11th century the years of Byzantine and Arab naval dominance were over. From that point on, what remained of their once formidable naval power would for the most part be used defensively, rather than in campaigns of conquest. Arab and Byzantine alike suffered from the repeated and rapacious attentions of the Italian city-states and their Crusading allies. The naval struggle which had raged across the Mediterranean for the best part of four centuries had finally come to an end, and with it the era of the *dromōn* and the *shalandī*.

FURTHER READING

George F. Bass, ed. (1972). *A History of Seafaring: Based on Underwater Archaeology.* London: Book Club Associates.

George F. Bass (1982). *Yassi Ada I: A Seventh Century Byzantine Shipwreck.* College Station, TX: Texas A&M University Press.

Lionel Casson (2014). *Ships and Seamanship in the Ancient World.* Princeton, NJ: Princeton University Press.

V. Christides (2002). 'Arab–Byzantine struggle in the sea: naval tactics (AD 7th–11th centuries): theory and practice', in Y.Y. al-Hijji & V. Christides, eds, *Aspects of Arab Seafaring: An Attempt to Fill in the Gap of Maritime History.* Athens: Institute for Graeco-Oriental and African Studies, pp. 87–101.

Aly Mohammed Fahmy (1966). *Muslim Naval Organisation in the Eastern Mediterranean from the Seventh to the Tenth Centuries AD.* Cairo: National Publication and Print House.

Robert Gardiner, ed. (1995). *The Age of the Galley: Mediterranean Oared Vessels since Pre-Classical Times.* London: Conway Maritime Press.

Thomas Glick, Steven Livesey & Faith Wallis, eds (2005). *Medieval Science, Technology and Medicine.* London: Routledge.

Molly Greene (2002). *A Shared World: Christians and Muslims in the Early Modern Mediterranean.* Princeton, NJ: Princeton University Press.

Archibald R. Lewis (1951). *Naval Power and Trade in the Mediterranean, AD 500–1100.* Princeton, NJ: Princeton University Press.

Archibald R. Lewis & Timothy J. Runyan (1985). *European Naval and Maritime History, 300–1500.* Bloomington, IN: Indiana University Press.

Adrienne Mayor (2003). *Greek Fire, Poison Arrow and Scorpion Bombs: Biological and Chemical Warfare in the Ancient World.* Woodstock, NY: Overlook Press.

Russell Meiggs (1982). *Trees and Timber in the Ancient Mediterranean World.* Oxford: Oxford University Press.

John Julius Norwich (1990). *Byzantium: The Early Centuries.* Harmondsworth: Penguin.

John Julius Norwich (1993). *Byzantium: The Apogee.* Harmondsworth: Penguin.

Michael Paul Pitassi (2012). *The Roman Navy: Ships, Men and Warfare, 350 BC–AD 475.* London: Seaforth Publishing.

John H. Pryor (1988). *Geography, Technology, and War: Studies in the Maritime History of the Mediterranean 649–1571.* Cambridge: Cambridge University Press.

John H. Pryor & Elizabeth M. Jeffreys (2006). *The Age of the Dromōn: The Byzantine Navy, c.500–1204.* Leiden: Koninklijke Brill.

Bill Sayer (2013). *Rowing and Sculling: The Complete Manual.* London: Robert Hale.

Timothy Shaw, ed. (1993). *The Trireme Project.* Oxbow Monographs 31. Oxford: Oxford University Press.

Theophanes the Confessor, ed. & trans. Harry Turtledove (1982). *The Chronicle of Theophanes.* Philadelphia, PA: University of Pennsylvania Press.

Speros Vryonis (1967). *Byzantium and Europe.* London: Thames & Hudson.

INDEX